FORWARD POEMS OF THE DECADE

A Guide for Edexcel AS/A Level English Literature
(8ET0/01 and 9ET0/03)

For GAX, her extraordinary English Department and the students, past and present, of The Langley Academy. Fun times!

About the Author

After graduating from Oxford University with a degree in English Language and Literature, and 26 years working for British Airways, I decided to train as a teacher of English. For the next ten years, I taught in the secondary state sector in a multi-cultural and socio-economically diverse area west of London. On my retirement in 2016, I was second in the English department, co-ordinator of the A Level English Literature curriculum and Lead Year 13 tutor, co-ordinating university entrance applications. I am an Examiner for AQA GCSE English Literature.

My approach to studying poetry is straightforward: unless you understand what is happening in the poem – the event, incident or story – about which the poet weaves his literary magic, there can be no understanding of a poet's literary techniques. The two are inextricably intertwined. There is a LOT of very variable analysis of poetry on the internet. Much of it stems from a failure to understand what is happening. This failure leaves students with a rattle-bag of literary terminology but with nothing on which to hang it. Naming metric forms and rhyme schemes, and poetic techniques such as assonance and sibilance, with no understanding of why the poet has used them, is a waste of time. It also leads to spurious, and erroneous, analysis of form and structure. I have read, in exam papers, that the "shape of the line on the page, if you turn it sideways, corresponds to the furrows of a field." Or, "the varied line length suggests the outline of the Manhattan skyline". Students do not come up with ideas like this unless there is a fundamental failure to grasp the links between substance (the "what is happening") and form (rhythm and rhyme) and language (the words used).

This guide is an attempt to make these links and help students appreciate why a poem has been written in the way that it has.

Contents

About this Guide

The Guide has been written primarily for students of AS and A Level English Literature as specified by Edexcel in the post-2015 syllabus (9ET0) Issue 3. It addresses Component 1 (8ET0/01 – Poetry and Drama) of the AS syllabus and Component 3 (9ET0/03 – Poetry) of the A2 syllabus, specifically, the requirement to study a selection of Post-2000 poetry.

The Guide covers all the poems in the revised selection from *Poems of the Decade: An Anthology of the Forward Books of Poetry 2002–2011* (ISBN 978-0571281732) as specified in Issue 3 of the Specification which takes effect from Summer 2018.

NOTE TO THE REVISED EDITION:

In 2016, the Edexcel Examination Board revised the selection of poems to be studied, **to take effect from Summer 2018**. Eight poems were removed from the selection. This version of the Guide has been updated to reflect these changes.

.
The Guide aims to address all the Assessment Objectives for the examination of this component, namely:

AO1 - Articulate creative, informed and relevant responses to literary texts, using appropriate terminology and concepts, and coherent, accurate written expression.

AO2 - Demonstrate detailed critical understanding in analysing the ways in which structure, form and language shape meanings in literary texts.

AO4 – Explore connections across literary texts.

The poems are explored individually, and links and connections between them are drawn as appropriate. The format of each exploration is similar:

- A summary of the key themes of the poems, with a note on possible connections and links to other poems in the selection
- An explanation of any key features of the poem that require additional contextual knowledge or illustration
- A brief summary of the metric form, rhyme scheme or other structural features
- A "walk-through" (or explication) of the poem, ensuring that what is happening in the poem is understood, how the rhythm and rhyme contribute to meaning, an explanation of the meaning of words which may be unfamiliar, an exploration of imagery and language and a comment on main themes.

A note on context

Whilst there is no requirement to have detailed knowledge of the biographical, social-economic, political or literary context in which these poems were written, it is important to know sufficient context to enable understanding of the poems. Understanding is enriched by knowing relevant autobiographical details, particularly where the subject matter focuses on familial relationships. Many of the poems use allusions and references to classical mythology, the Bible, popular culture and general knowledge, without which meaning is obscure and appreciation limited. Where context is considered essential to aid understanding, or where it is felt that students might be interested in acquiring a broader understanding, it has been included in the exploration of the poems. In addition, Edexcel has published a high-level commentary on each of these poems which includes biographical details of the authors as a *Guide for Teachers*", to which students are advised to refer.

A note on "appropriate terminology" (AO1)

This means the use of the semantic field of literary criticism – or "jargon". Criticism has a language to describe the features peculiar to the study of literature, just as football has words to describe manoeuvres and equipment – *"penalty"*, *"off-side"*, *"wing"*, *"long cross"*, *"throw-in"*. To be able to critique literature, you need to know this language and use it correctly. Throughout this guide, literary terminology has been *italicised*, indicating that these words need to become part of your vocabulary when discussing the texts and writing essays. For illustration, here are some very basic literary terms that are often carelessly used and will lose you marks in the exam if you do not apply them correctly.

Text – is the printed words. The *whole text* is all the words that are identified, usually by a *title*, as belonging together as an integral piece of writing.

A *Book* is a collection of printed pages bound together to make a *whole text*. A *book* can be any text – fiction, non-fiction; play, novel; car maintenance manual, encyclopaedia. A *book* is a **physical** entity, like *"DVD"* or *"scroll"*, not a creative one.

A *novel* is a particular kind of text – a *genre*. It is characterised by certain creative features, such as being *fictional*, usually *narrative in structure* and with various *characters* who do things, or have things happen to them. It may be *descriptive*, and may contain *dialogue*.

A *play* is another *genre*. It is designed to be performed and watched, rather than read. It can be *fictional* or *non-fictional*, or a mixture. It is predominantly made up of *dialogue* between *characters*, although there may be descriptive elements within this *dialogue* and in the *stage directions*.

A *poem* is a particular *genre* which is characterised by the deliberate, and recurring, use of *rhythm* and *rhyme* and/or by a particular attention to *diction*, in the form of *word-choice* and *imagery*. It is opposed to *prose*. However, there are *poetical prose* writers whose language uses the distinctive features of poetry – such as *alliteration, rhythm* and *imagery*.

Beyond these simple definitions, there are a host of other literary terms. These terms have been used where they are necessary to describe features of the texts and are defined on the first usage, and subsequently when repeated, depending on how common the usage and the relevance to the poem under discussion.

A note on "shape meaning" (AO2)

There are very few marks to be gained by simply spotting and correctly naming literary techniques. Comments on literary techniques **must** be linked to purpose and meaning to gain marks in the higher bands. This principle has been followed in the analyses of the texts. See the section *"About the Author"* for a further comment on the dangers of spotting literary techniques in isolation from the meaning of the text. Not all literary techniques used receive a comment; only those that are particularly relevant to the discussion of meaning, form or theme have been explored. Further guidance on this is given in the section on *"Links and Connections."*

A note on "connections" (AO4)

The new specification marks a shift from making "comparisons" between literary texts (as in the old syllabus) to making *"links and connections"*. This avoids the student having to make, often spurious, comparisons which fail to illuminate the text, and the tedium of essays structured around *"on the one hand/ on the other"*. It does, however, challenge the student to be able to *synthesise* their knowledge of the texts – a higher level skill. Further guidance on this is given in the section on *"Links and Connections"*.

A note on "themes"

The question in the AS level examination for *Component 1– Poetry and Drama – Section A - Post-2000 Poetry* (8ET0/01) will be on a *"theme"* – a central concern or idea which may form the focus of the poem or be an integral part of its meaning. You will be asked to explore the presentation of this *"theme"* in one named poem and one other poem of your choice.

At A Level, for *Component 3 – Poetry – Section A – Post-2000 Poetry* (9ET0/3), the question will ask you to explore the presentation of a given *"theme"* in a poem of your choice from the selection and link it to the treatment of the same *theme* in an Unseen poem.

These "themes" could include, but not be limited to: an **emotion** – such as love, loss, sorrow, joy; the **evocation of "place"**, as the subject of the poem, or as the setting for the poem; the treatment of **abstract concepts** such as Time, or Death, or Religion; a **"happening"** such as War, Childhood, Marriage; the **relationships between men and women**. The range is very broad.

Where a poem lends itself to suggesting a particular theme, this has been noted in the overview and linked to other poems which have similar themes. However, these suggestions are illustrative, not exhaustive; one of the skills to be mastered is to know the texts well enough to be able to link them to themes which may not be immediately obvious. Students should spend some time mapping the links between poems thematically, and illustrating how these themes are treated in similar or differing ways.

As well as links of *theme,* links and connections can be made between *narrative voice, form, structure* and *language.* At the end of this book are some questions which should be considered when making links and connections, and when analysing the Unseen. (See *"Making Links and Connections."*)

Preparing for the Unseen Poem for A Level (9ET0/03)

The best preparation for this component of the examination is to read poetry, of all kinds, regularly. There are a number of websites which will deliver a *"poem-a-day"* to your mobile. These two combine contemporary American poetry with classics:

https://www.poets.org/poetsorg/poem-day
https://www.poetryfoundation.org/newsletter

In addition to this, Edexcel/Pearson have published an *"Unseen Poetry Preparation Anthology"* available for download on the Edexcel website, of which you should have a copy. This contains four perspectives on tackling the Unseen element of the exam plus exemplar material for practice.

How to use this Guide

As the poems within the selection are copyrighted to the authors, it has not been possible to print them within this Guide. You will therefore need to read the commentaries with a copy of the text alongside. However, the poems have been quoted in places for illustrative purposes.

Generally, each paragraph of the commentary corresponds to a stanza, unless otherwise indicated. Reference has been made to *stanzas* and *line numbers* when referring to particular parts of the texts, based on the version of the poems as published by Forward in the prescribed text.

THE POEMS

Eat Me – Patience Agbabi

We are bombarded in the media by images of "the perfect body". Well-known high street stores, that cater for women of all ages, use size 8 models, even though the average dress size for women in the UK is 16. Teenage girls (and boys, but to a lesser extent) are increasingly suffering from body "dysmorphia" – a debilitating psychological condition in which sufferers develop the belief that some aspect of their appearance is defective in some way. The number of teenagers hospitalised for eating disorders doubled between 2012 and 2015; it has been described as "a silent epidemic." Whilst women's body shape has always been a subject for scrutiny and comment, as well as reverence, "Size Zero" has not always been regarded as an ideal. Classical figures of women show them as curvaceous. Women in the paintings of Paul Ruben's (17th century) could be described as positively roly-poly. In parts of the world, large women were revered for their voluptuous body shape – for rounded buttocks, large breasts and thighs – as a sign of fertility and are depicted in the images of their goddesses. There are signs that the extreme thinness seen as desirable in the early 2000s is being replaced by a healthier, and more realistic, depiction of female body shape, partly in response to the popularity of female icons such as Beyoncé.

Agbabi's poem addresses notions of **Self** and **Identity**, linking it with *"Genetics"* and *"Out of the Bag"*. It considers **Sexual Politics** as in *"Chainsaw Versus the Pampas Grass"* and *"The Gun"*. In its use of rhythm and rhyme, it can be linked to *"Genetics", and "Out of the Bag"* which are also written in *tercets*[1]. The use of *enjambment*[2] and *caesura* can be linked to *"Out of the Bag"*, both

---

[1]A *tercet* is a three- line stanza
[2]*Enjambment* – running the sense of a line over from the end of one line onto the next, often with an emphasis on the first word of the succeeding line. Used with *caesura* to vary the effect of a regular rhyme

10

using the technique to propel the poem forward within the use of regular rhyme and rhythm. "*Eat Me*" uses religious imagery, as does "*Out of the Bag*". It is also one of a number of *dramatic monologues*[3] in the selection.

In spite of the modernity of the subject matter, the poem is written in traditional form using both rhythm and rhyme. Each stanza is a *tercet* and the rhythm is predominantly *iambic tetrametre*[4], with four stressed beats to a line, which gives it a forward impetus. The regular rhythm is varied by extensive use of *enjambment*, which helps to create the "voice" of the *persona* as she relates her story. Agbabi also makes subtle use of rhyme and *half-rhyme*[5] in the first and third lines of each stanza, which give the poem a purposeful tone – this is not an idle reminiscence, but a story which has a beginning, middle and end, being told by a victim who gets her revenge.

The *persona* of this *dramatic monologue* is a woman in a long-term relationship with a man who is an *adipophiliac* or "fat fetishist" (a man who is sexually attracted to large women), and a *feeder,* one who feeds his partner to make them bigger. Stanza 1 opens with "*When I hit thirty*", as if it were referring to her thirtieth birthday – traditionally a milestone birthday in a person's life, as they approach middle-age. We then realise that the number is a milestone because she has "*hit*" 30 stone in weight (190.5 kgs). The word "*hit*" suggests that this is a target aimed for, and now celebrated, by the partner with the ironically decorated three-layered "*cake*". This is not a celebration of a

---

and/or rhythm.
[3] A *dramatic monologue* is poem "spoken" in the voice of a *persona* who is not the poet.
[4] *Iambic tetrametre* – a line of four stressed beats, predominantly of *iambic* (*ti-TUM*) metric feet.
[5] *Half-rhyme or near rhyme* – words that have similar, but not identical, sounds.

11

natural aging process, but of an unnatural development in an unhealthy relationship. "30 BMI" is the mark at which a person is classified by the National Health Service as being "obese" – a boundary crossed between "normal" and "abnormal".

The cake is traditionally decorated in "white" and "pink", suggestive of both innocence and femininity, and with the words "Eat Me" - the instruction to Alice in Wonderland. This story, written in the late 19th century by Lewis Carroll (Charles Dodgson), describes how Alice travels through Wonderland, at times eating or drinking cakes and potions which change her size – and only by doing so can she enter the next phase of the story, as if she undergoes successive "rites of passage". However, this stanza gives us the first hint that the feedee is not an entirely passive victim – or may not remain so – as she "did/what I was told" and "doesn't even taste it". She retains sufficient objectivity – if not will – to recognise that what is happening to her is not consensual.

The feeder asks the woman to perform a kind of ritual "dance" whilst he watches the physical manifestation of his actions. Agbabi uses alliteration and the enjambment between broad/belly wobble and the alliteration and assonance of "judder like a juggernaut" to emphasise her physical size and, by using the simile of a large truck, she has become fetishised, and dehumanised, losing her individuality.

In stanza 4, we hear the partner's voice, opening with a cliché – "the bigger the better" - and then generalising his preferences, further dehumanising her. The word "burrow" is animalistic, as well as sexual, as he buries himself in the underground of her flesh, like a creature coming home to find sustenance, and safety. The abundance of her solace is evident from the words "multiple" and "masses". She is bountiful in her giving, like a fertility goddess.

The idea of the man being enveloped by the woman is continued in the 5th stanza with the image of the *"Jacuzzi"* – a bubbling cauldron of water that is also a modern symbol of excess and sexual pleasure. The woman recognises their mutual dependency – he takes pleasure from her, but she is addicted to the food that he - *"her cook"* – provides, laden as it is, like *"fast food"* from a takeaway, with fat and sugar. Although his pleasure remains sexual, hers lies solely in a *"sugar rush"*. *"forbidden fruit"* is a biblical reference to the apple in the Garden of Eden, which, if eaten, gave knowledge of good and evil. This is ironic, as he has tasted of this fruit many times.

The next stanza is linked by developing the idea of *"fruit"* to refer, possibly, to the couples' ethnicity and a famous story. *"Breadfruit"*, originating in the Pacific, was introduced to the Caribbean in the 18th century and then to other tropical regions, including Africa, where it is widely grown today. It is prized for its high nutritional value and heavy cropping, and is now considered a modern "superfood". It is also famous for its role in the "Mutiny on the *Bounty*", an incident in the late 18th century, when an expedition sent from England to transport breadfruit from Tahiti in the Pacific to the slave colonies in the Caribbean, underwent a mutiny of the crew. Captain Bligh was set adrift in a boat with few men and provisions while the mutinous crew headed, with the HMS *Bounty,* back to Tahiti. Some eleven months and 3,800 miles later, Captain Bligh, against all odds, arrived back in England. Many of the deserting crew were subsequently rounded up in Tahiti and hanged some months later. Christian Fletcher, the leader of the mutineers, remained lost for twenty years, before an American ship landed at Pitcairn Island in the South Pacific, to be met by a man who claimed to be the last surviving crew member from the Bounty and that Fletcher had been killed some years previously. The current inhabitants of the Pitcairn islands, a British dependency, all trace their ancestry back to Fletcher and his crew. This nautical tale may be referenced in the idea of a *"desert island after shipwreck"*. It is also a pun on *"dessert"* meaning pudding. The nautical theme is continued with the image of the woman as a *"beached whale"*, a slang reference to a fat woman who has trouble getting up from a prone position, who craves *"a wave"* to enable her to move. In the idea of *"a tidal wave of flesh"* she becomes not an inhabitant of the sea, but the sea itself, overwhelming and irresistible.

Enjambment links stanzas 6 and 7, transitioning from woman as wave to woman as flesh. She has reached a stage in her growth where she is no longer able to move or leave her house – even to go out for a pint of milk. She can no longer pretend that how she is, is normal. The excuses and *euphemisms*[6] for being obese, *"chubby, cuddly, big-built"* no longer convince.

Stanza 8 records another milestone, another target *"hit"*. 39 BMI is "morbidly obese", with danger of death. However, she appears to have reached some kind of goddess-like status, where she now has the power, as she "allows" him to *"stroke the globe of a cheek"*. The *"globe"* suggests a universality – she has become more than a fat woman trapped in an unhealthy relationship, and achieved mythical status. Their bodily form has given way to an incorporeal state and they *"flow"* together. The act of eating has been supplanted by giving libations – liquid offerings to the goddess in the form of the *"olive oil"*.

Her partner looks forward to the next milestone (*forty*), and, as if in acceptance of his prayer, she responds with a gift – the whole of her rolling over and giving the whole of herself to him in the *"tidal wave of flesh"*. In so doing she *"drowns"* - smothers - him.

The final stanza sees the tables turned. Unable to move, with the dead body of the partner below her, she rests. There is black humour in the *"felt like a week"*, which we use to describe a short

---

[6] *Euphemism* – a word which attempts to soften the meaning, such as *"passed away"* for *"dead"*.

time that seems to pass slowly. *"Six hours"* and *"felt like a week"* may also develop the religious imagery and refer to the six days that it took God to create the world, and on the seventh day, he rested. In her circumstances, it **is** a long time. Below her, the dead man, eyes *"bulging"*, gazes forever at the thing he desired and worshipped and to which he has become the sacrifice. Her greed has become his greed. But his death leaves her unfed – she cannot move, cannot get help. She is hungry. We are left with the unspoken realisation that the *feeder* is about to become the *food*. She has *"turned the tables"* on her abuser.

Chainsaw Versus the Pampas Grass – Simon Armitage

Simon Armitage is a poet whose poetry is often autobiographical and rooted in his personal life – his boyhood, his family and the North of England where he grew up and still lives. Armitage does write *dramatic monologues*, and it is possible that this is one. However, it seems more likely, with its domestic setting and its strongly realised detail of the shed and the garden, that the speaker is the poet. In *dramatic monologues*, the focus is on the *persona* of the speaker. Here, the focus is firmly on the instrument of destruction – the chainsaw.

The poem is variously explained as being about the relationships between **Men and Women**, (linking it to *"Eat Me"* and *"The Gun"*), **Man and Nature**, **Man and Mortality** (linking it to *"Ode…"* and *"Effects"*). All of these themes, and more, are contained in the use of *extended metaphor*[7] in his portrayal of the chainsaw as a male stereotype and the pampas grass as a female, so it is legitimate to say that it is not about just one idea but many. It is also a dramatic and visually detailed account of a man cutting down some pampas grass. Much of the strength of the poem lies in this close dovetailing of the literal and the figurative in the use of language and choice of imagery. In this use of *extended metaphor*, the poem can be linked with *"An Easy Passage"*.

The poem is written in *free verse* – it does not have a regular rhythm or rhyme scheme. That is not to say, however, that it lacks either rhythm or rhyme entirely. The rhythm comes from the choice of where to break the line and from the use of techniques such as *assonance*[8], *consonance*[9] and *alliteration*[10].

---

[7] *Extended metaphor* - a similarity between two things which is continued and developed over a number of points of comparison
[8] *Assonance* – rhyming or similar sounding vowels

The aural effect of the choice of line breaks is best appreciated if the poem is read out loud – Armitage's poetry, capturing, as it does, the cadences of speech, can best be appreciated by recitation. The line breaks also enable Armitage to juxtapose surprising images to bring force to his narrative. The momentary pause at the end of lines "sets up" the initial word of the next, with dramatic effect.

The title of the poem announces that it is about a contest, and the first line tells us how unlikely a match it is. But, as in Agbabi's poem, there is a hint that our expectations of the outcome will be thwarted in the use of the word "seemed". As we learn, appearances can be deceptive. The chainsaw, the *dramatis persona*[11] of the poem, is personified as a stereotypical male through the use of male-oriented colloquialisms. It is frustrated by being left idle – *unplugged* - all winter and grinds its "teeth" impotently, hidden away and out of reach in its prison, suggested by the word "hatch". Like a prisoner thirsting for light, or a man for a beer, it drinks quickly, the liquid giving it new life and energy. Armitage's use of line breaks can be seen in "can/it knocked back", shifting from the literal (oil from a can) to the *personification*[12] of the chainsaw as a thirsty man.

The second stanza contains images of earlier deaths in the "wreckage of wasps and flies", a pre-cursor of what is to come and introducing the **theme of mortality**. The idea of the latent destructive power in the chainsaw is contained in the simile "like powder from a keg" to describe the trailing power-line. The actions of the narrator are described in laconic detail – the walking to and fro, the flicking of the power-switch, the joining of

---

[9] *Consonance* – rhyming or similar sounding consonants
[10] *Alliteration* – repeating letters at the beginning of consecutive, or nearby, words for effect
[11] *Dramatis persona* - character
[12] *Personification* is attributing human characteristics to objects

the power source to the chainsaw, taking off the safety catch, - building up to the explosion that occurs when he *"guns"* the trigger, the electricity bringing the monster to life.

There is more than a hint of a Frankenstein moment in the *"instant rage"* that the chainsaw exhibits. It is ready to kill from the start, *"lashing out"* blindly, the narrator having to fight for control. It is inhuman, careless of human life, focused solely on destruction. The use of *"cloth, or jewellery, or hair"* as the chainsaw's potential target introduces the idea of a **conflict between men and women.** This idea develops with the description of the chainsaw having *"desire"* and a *"sweet tooth"* (meaning it likes sweet things), introducing a sexual element. The line break after *"tooth"*, however, shifts us to imagery of blood and a desire to "eat" its victims flesh and bones which is also suggestive of the chainsaw as the **image of Death.** This is reinforced if you remember that Death is known in folk lore as "The Grim Reaper" – precisely what this chainsaw is about to do in combating the pampas grass. The idea of the chainsaw as being alive is further developed in that it has a "plan", it will stop at nothing to get to its victim. The narrator's familiarity with the machine is conveyed by reference to *"nail or knot"* which can cause the chainsaw to buck in the hands of the operator and lose control, as of a wild horse. But the narrator keeps it under control and "allows" it to feel the freedom of light and air while he enjoys the feeling of being in command of the latent power in the *"drumming...heart"* and inhuman sounds it makes.

Attention now switches abruptly to the opponent in the opposite corner – the pampas grass. We move from a masculine to a feminine lexis[13]. It is described as showy and extravagant, with redundant ornamentation in its *"ludicrous"* feathery plumes. Not only that, but it is vain and selfish. It denies the plants around it

---

[13] *Lexis* = vocabulary

"*warmth and light*", spreading itself luxuriously like a pampered (the ghost of a pun here?) woman sitting sunbathing surrounded by pool cushions. Except – it has "*twelve-foot spears*". Armitage uses the line break to put this at the end of the stanza, to give us pause. This is not an entirely helpless image of femininity. This woman is armed to the teeth. Not only that, but the "*spears*" are phallic. Grass has been used as a phallic symbol in poetry before – most notably in Walt Whitman's collection "*Leaves of Grass*", of which Armitage is unlikely to be unaware. So, we have here the masculine and feminine combined. This would suggest that the pampas grass is an image of **Mother Nature** or of **Mankind** itself. It now appears over-simplistic to focus on this poem as only about men versus women.

On the surface, however, the use of the chainsaw to tackle this fragile-looking plant seems over the top. Armitage uses the cliché of the "*sledgehammer*" to show confidence in his/the chainsaw's ability to take the plant down, reinforced by the word "*Overkill*". He seems almost embarrassed by his eagerness to get out the chainsaw to do the job. The delicacy with which he approaches his first cut confirms this hesitation, and the imbalance between the instrument of destruction and its victim is emphasised in the result; it does not merely cut – it annihilates its opponent. The power now made visible excites the narrator – notice the increasingly strong verbs: *touched, dabbed, docked, dismissed, sweep.* This isn't a contest – this is a "*game*". Increasingly confident, and violent, he lets the chainsaw loose on the "*trunk*", the centre of the plant. The imagery becomes visceral – "blood" spurts from the "organs" of the plant as if from a human body. The equivalence between man-with-chainsaw and murderer is completed with this *metaphor*. The plant is again feminised in the "*dark, secret warmth*" suggestive of female genitalia.

Matter-of-factly, the man clears up the mess of his "murder", the wholesale destruction evident in the "*severed*", "*felled*", "*torn*".

This stanza reasserts the masculine, this time literally, as the man clears away the debris in a methodical and organised fashion, preparing the debris for burning. Yet, he is not quite satisfied with his efforts at annihilating the pampas grass. An annoying "*stump*" remains which is impervious to the chainsaw, magically resisting his efforts to make further inroads into its secret heart. His efforts are futile. As a last gesture, he attempts to set fire to it, but gives up. He thinks he has done enough.

In the weeks to come, he discovers just how resistant the plant is to his efforts at its destruction. New asparagus "*spears*", green and tender now, but with the potential to grow, appear from its "*nest*", an image of nurturing. It is soon exhibiting all the jaunty confidence it did before, reasserting its dominance – in control, reigning over the garden. "*crown*" is used here both literally and metaphorically. "*Corn in Egypt*" is a reference to the Bible. The Nile floods every year, bringing apparent desolation, but from beneath the flood waters, the corn springs up every spring. In the book of Genesis, the starving Canaanites send Jacob to Joseph in Egypt to beg for corn. They do not recognise him as the brother they sold into slavery years before and Joseph denies them corn until they bring him a hostage. "*Corn in Egypt*" has become a symbol of bounty in a time of scarcity. The man looks out at the resurgence of the plant as uselessly as the moon shines at midday in the presence of the sun.

The man's feeling of impotence in the face of this new growth is shared by the personified chainsaw, which "*seethes*" in anger at its failure, confined to its prison once again. The man decides to leave it until next year to "*learn*" a lesson – one that he, too, temporarily forgot in his pride and the confidence he placed in a mere "*man-made*" machine, and hence, artificial, weapon. In contrast, "*grass*" – specifically the pampas grass, but more generally **Nature,** never forgot that it would come back, seemingly from the dead. The chainsaw gets no further in its musings than a realisation of an *"urge"* in Nature to keep going, but no understanding of *why*.

By the end of the poem, in the man's message to the chainsaw, and us, it seems that there are two linked themes, which are arguably the same. The first is that Death may come to man individually, but Mankind continues, in its offspring. This interpretation would be supported by the image of Death as The Grim Reaper, the feminising of the plant and the image of the "nest". Closely aligned is the idea of the indestructibility of Mother Nature, in the face of man's destructive tendencies.

Material – Ros Barber

This is one of a number of autobiographical poems in the selection that **explores the relationship between adult children and their parents.** Other poems to which *"Material"* can be thematically linked include *"The Deliverer"*, *"Genetics"*, *"Out of the Bag"*, *"Effects"*, and *"On Her Blindness"*. The poem also explores **Memory, the effects of Time,** the **changing role of women and society** and **the nature of the creative process.**

Where the parents being recalled are dead, the poems could be referred to as *elegies* – poems that mourn the death of a loved one whilst praising them and, ultimately, finding some solace or reconciliation in the act of remembrance. *"Effects"* and *"On Her Blindness"* could be considered *elegies* as they commemorate the dead.

The poem is written in eight-line stanzas of *iambic tetrametre* with a rhyming pattern of *abcb* which is sustained throughout, using both full and *half-rhymes* and *assonance*. This gives the poem a fairly tight structure – the reminiscences have purpose and a forward momentum; there is a certain defiance in her memories of her childhood and her mother, as if she is insisting on the need to let go of the past and move on in the present.

The title suggests these multiple thematic concerns. *"Material"* is both the fabric out of which the handkerchiefs are made, that are the trigger point for the poem, and the stuff of the poem itself – the memories and reminiscences about the life she shared with her mother and the life she now shares with her children. If something is *"material"* it also *matters,* is important. Her handkerchief means more to her mother than a piece of useful cloth – it is a symbol of how you live a decent life. The poet is well aware of how manners, behaviours, and perhaps values, have changed since her mother was young and the poet was a child, and she looks back on her mother's life with a mixture of nostalgia and regret, as well as a hint of exasperation and perhaps resentment. The handkerchief is a symbol of a lost world and a lost life. Ironically, it is also *immaterial* (unimportant) in the face of her mother's death.

The poem opens with a tribute to her mother, the *"hanky queen"*, who is never seen without one. The word *"hanky"* has an old-fashioned ring to it now, although use of that word by the daughter would have seemed like modern slang to her mother. But Time has moved on again to the disposable *"tissue"*. The contrast between the mother's lifestyle and the grown-up daughter's is captured in the image of her mother waving farewell from a train and the suppression of grief in drying tears in the corners of your eyes, possibly images from the Second World War. This contrasts with the disposable, fast-moving pace of the modern world where packs of tissues are bought in an emergency or as an afterthought, and a society which, perhaps, displays its grief openly and unashamedly. In her mother's day, *"hankies were material"* – a *pun* meaning that they were made of cloth, and they mattered.

The second stanza branches out from the memory of her mother's *"hanky"* tucked up the sleeve of her *"cardi"* – the old-fashioned slang word capturing the mother's and her childhood language – to recall her experiences as a child. The *"hanky"* is embroidered with her mother's initials and has a lace edge – an embarrassing, dated fashion for a young girl brought up in the 60s. Even worse, it is used to clean the child's face. There is humour in her image of the hankies mating up her mother's sleeve, as the child is unable to figure out where they come from, the humour pointed up by the rhyme on *"there/squares"*.

Her mother is of an era where you would go and buy handkerchiefs routinely, but the child is of a different generation and regards these gifts from aunts with something like disdain. She sees them as affected – *"ponce"* is a word meaning effeminate or "stuck up" – and deeply "uncool". Again, Barber uses contemporary slang to characterise voice and time (as does Turnbull in *"Ode…"*). She is sarcastic about the fact that her brothers also received hankies – big masculine ones – a reminder of how gender difference was literally built into the fabric of her mother's society.

In stanza 4, her reminiscences on the Christmas gifts lead her further to reflect on handkerchiefs as a symbol of changes in wider society. Handkerchiefs were among the staple products that used to be sold in the old haberdashery departments of the department stores – large stores that sold a wide variety of goods for the home, as well as clothes. Some have survived – Debenham's, Selfridge's, House of Fraser, John Lewis – but many have ceased trading, as the goods they provided fell out of fashion and the stores gave way to shopping malls. Hankies were also of a time when women were largely confined to the home and able to spend time washing and ironing them.

Not only have the department stores disappeared, but so too have shops which delivered; she cites the greengrocer but so have the milkman, the coalman, and the Corona man who sold fizzy drinks from a truck. The individual traders, such as butchers and fishmongers have gone too, all now superseded by supermarkets. She seems to suggest, in her detailing of the *"dodgy foot"* and *"friendly butcher"*, as well as the *"painted talons"* of the dancing teacher in the next stanza, that with the demise of these trades, there has been a loss of individuality and possibly, humanity.

Memories seem now to come in a stream; the marked *enjambment* across stanzas 4 and 5, moves us visually and narratively across the road from the *fishmonger* to the *dancing school* opposite where Mrs White's pupils practise for the Annual Talent Show. The hanky again does its duty in exerting a mother's control over her daughters, in toning down the make-up put on their cheeks.

The next stanza brings an abrupt change of mood. She breaks off from her reminiscences, as if she has been day-dreaming and comes back suddenly to the here and now, finding herself amongst her own children - yet another generation with its own concerns and values, which are not hers. Looking back has made her realise not only the passage of her own time, but how life will go on changing, as evident from her own children and her relationship with them. On the one hand, she would like them to have the kind of innocent childhood that she had – but she realises, perhaps with a touch of resentment or even bitterness, that such a wish is as futile and out-of-date as the now defunct sterling – the *"ten-bob notes"* as they were called when she was a child. The media has destroyed childhood innocence – and she is guilty, as it is she that has *"turned it on"*. With this we are brought into the present time, into the act of her writing this poem. She contrasts her mothering with that of her mother's; she is a working woman who buys biscuits rather than baking them and turns on the TV to keep the kids quiet. There is a sense here of what has been lost in the demands placed on the modern woman.

In stanza 8, Barber further examines her own mothering skills, and comes up wanting. Her kids are not neatly turned out and she never has a hanky handy. She finds herself not quite able to adapt to using disposable tissues and acknowledges nostalgia for the material ones of her mother's which gave her access to memory and hence to her and her mother's shared *"history"*.

Finally, however, she rejects the temptation to stay in the past – she'll *"let it go"*. She acknowledges that her mother, too, in dying, had to let things go – even having to use disposable tissues. But the poet is dissatisfied. The *"scratchy and disposable"* seems to refer both to the tissues, to her unkempt children and to the uncomfortable and unsatisfactory end of a life (echoing the *"uncertainty"* of the earlier line). The poem ends with an echo of the mother's voice as she tries to comfort her daughter by telling her that the time is now hers to live and that she must make what she will of it. The *material* the poet has to work with can be taken as memory, as the "stuff" or source of her poetry, as well as her own children's lives, much as her mother worked on the material of her daughter's life.

The "uncertainty" of the end of the poem echoes the end of "*On Her Blindness*", and "*Effects*", as if the "children" fail to find solace in the death of their mothers. They are left with a sense of things unsaid or business unfinished, as well as guilt.

History – John Burnside

This is potentially the hardest poem in the collection to understand. As an introduction, and some further help, go to: http://26project.org.uk/commonground/2010/03/23/wet-sand-and-gasoline/ or http://www.scottishpoetrylibrary.org.uk/poetry/poets/john-burnside .

This poem can be linked to *"Ode to a GP Urn"* in exploring **Time**; *"The Lammas Hireling"* or *"Guiseppe"* in exploring an **alternative reality**; *"Out of the Bag"* on the **power of Imagination**; poems on **Identity**, such as *"A Minor Role"* or even *"An Easy Passage"*, as the latter is about the transition between child and woman; **parents and children** and the ties that bind them together, as in *"Material"* and **the creative process** as in *"Material"*. It also has a strongly realised **Setting** or sense of **Place**.

The poem was written within a few weeks of *9/11* and this was its original title. The title *"History"* came later. It is not clear that Burnside means "History" as we would understand it. He has an approach to time and the "now" which is peculiar to him. Burnside has been described as being interested in the *liminal* - which literally means threshold or doorway, and in the poem, means in-between and transitional states of being. This could be understood as what lies between reality and imagination, or our concept of time (which is not fixed, but changes constantly), between the names we give things and the thing itself. It reads as a series of linked thoughts which range between 9/11, the child on the beach and the kite flying, whilst reflecting on the nature of reality and time, through an evocation of the landscape.

The version in the Forward anthology is not the same as that originally published. The original did not have the same punctuation nor line lengths - these seem to have been edited by Burnside for publication in the Forward anthology. This makes some commentary on this poem highly questionable, where it attempts to link the visual layout of the poem with the Twin Towers or Manhattan skyline. This version of the poem has a strong *iambic* beat and, although the lines are frequently broken visually, much is written in combinations of loose *iambic pentametres* and *tetrametres*[14]. The breaking lines seem to indicate the associative nature of his thinking – moving between what he sees and does on the beach and the context of this day in the wider world. The more regular rhythm and line lengths occur, as in stanza 4 and 6, where he tries to capture his thoughts on what this might mean to him and his child.

The poem is rich in detailed description and imagery, of the rock pools and water, which gives it layers of meaning and a sensory appeal, as well as being intellectually challenging. In this it could be linked to the description of the Doctor's nightmare laboratory in *"Out of the Bag"*.

The poem is set on a beach in Burnside's native Scotland, near the Royal St Andrew's golf course (the *"golf links"* referred to) on a windy day when he and his son, Lucas, are exploring the seashore while parents (and he possibly includes himself in this by the use of *"we"*) are flying kites. The scene is intensely realised, appealing to the sense of sight and smell; the wind is whipping up the dry sand on the beach and it streams in *"ribbons"*; the colour of the sea is particularised by reference to a *"quail"*, a small, mottled gamebird. On the breeze comes the smell of aviation fuel from the nearby RAF base, Leuchars. Following the 9/11 atrocity, there is heightened activity from the base and people stop to watch the aircraft on manoeuvres overhead. The aircraft call 9/11 to mind and with it the feeling of dread, which he has tried to suppress (*"muffled"*) since it happened. Burnside is experiencing the feeling that many people had after 9/11, that this was the beginning of something much bigger and potentially worse, which it proved to be.

---

[14] *Pentametre* is a five stressed, tetrametre is a *four stressed,* line

Perhaps to reassure himself that all will be well, and retain a semblance of normality, the poet focuses on his son *"gathering shells/ and pebbles"*. Even here, however, images of 9/11 intrude. The *"finding evidence of life in all this / driftwork"* and *"shreds/smudges/flesh"* is a reminder of how the emergency services sifted through the wreckage of the Twin Towers to find the remains of victims.

The poet then stops to try and summarise his thoughts on identity – *"what makes us who we are"*. This is not simply our families, or nationality, or genes – the things we inherit. (*"states"* may be a pun on "United States"). Giving names to things is how we make them real. He suggests that there is something beyond naming, which gets *"lost"*. He then uses the metaphor of the *"kite"* to try and explain what he means. Our bodies are on the ground (*"fixed and anchored"*) but we are flying our *kites*, tethered to us by a *"line"*, the kite strings, that stretch between us on the ground and the kite in the sky. Our sense of self, or our identity, lies, like the *"lines"*, in the *"space between"* - between what we perceive in this world as our reality, and what lies just beyond our grasp, in the spaces between reality and imagination. This is an instance of Burnside's interest in *"liminal spaces"* – the spaces between things.

This idea is further explored in the next stanza. *"Property"* are the things we own, but also can be interpreted as the *"properties of matter"*– what makes us solid, and mortal, – referring back to the idea of us being *"anchored"* or fixed in our bodies. *"Tethered"* means tied down, as the kite is tethered by the string to the person holding it. *"Gravity"* and *"light"* are opposites – one of the earth, the other of the sky – and he is suggesting that we inhabit the space in between – a space made up of *"distance and shapes"* – things which are intangible, but nevertheless visible to us.

We can learn about these intangibles by reading from *"the book of nature"* as he sees now before him as he beachcombs with his son. *"Tides"* are movements – they are not real, in the sense that an object is real and susceptible to the senses. They are a concept based on our ideas about time. *Silt* is what is left behind as the *tides* come and go – they are the remains of time. He examines the inhabitants of a rock pool, capturing the varied colours and shapes. The images are of fragility – jellyfish are soft-bodied, as are sea anemones, and as his son's childish, naked body.

These images of beauty and fragility lead him to musing on the transitory nature of what we perceive to be our real world. Once again, the lines become shorter, more focused, and in regular *iambic tetrametre* as he strives to capture the ideas that his observations have prompted. He is *"dizzy"*, disorientated, as he looks at the world around him and realises that this world is only *"virtual"* – almost, but not quite real. We hold onto tangible realities and we think that things that we have *"named"* and are made of *"matter"* or have *"properties"*, (the words he used in the previous stanza) are real – but they are not. There are *"other bodies"* – things which are illusory or intangible – like *tides*, that *"drift and tug"*, and the shifting patterns *"of light and weather"* – and that we should be aware of, as they impact us, even if we do not recognise them or realise their importance at the time that they happen or *"shift"*.

This *"shift"* is history. We think of history as time passed – but it is in fact being created in the present – in the space between the past and the future. He illustrates this idea with images of fish, *"lodged"*, as if held timelessly, in the movement of the tides. Similarly, the carp (large fish of the goldfish family) appear to be caught between sleeping and waking (*"insomnia"*) and are also *"hung"* in the water. Seamus Heaney uses a similar image of fish *"hanging"* in a stream in his poem *"Perch"*, which is also a meditation on the nature of time passing. *"Transitive"* means *"in transit"* – being carried between one place and another – presumably between life and death. The image of the *"spawn"* is another *"transitive"* state, between egg and frog, and a symbol of potential – something which will be, but is not yet. *"Sticklebacks"* are small fish which children used to catch to bring home to keep, and *"goldfish"* were given away as prizes to children at fairgrounds. They are, literally, *"fish out of (their natural) water"* and caught between states. The reference to the *"hum of radio"* harks back to the time of this childhood, when the radio was kept permanently on, and suggests that these are his own memories. And memory is itself a *liminal state*, between *now* and *then*.

In the final lines, he asks how we can live in and interact with this fragile world, without altering it or harming it. (Burnside is a keen Eco politician.) He recaps the central images of the poem – the child and the parents flying kites, as examples of people attempting to do just that – understand their world and take from it what is valuable, but intangible: their feelings for their child. The child attempts to make sense of what he sees before him and understand what he cannot see, while the parents watch him anxiously. *"Plugged"* suggests that they are firmly attached to what they understand or know, and to the child, but even so their *"line"* reaches skywards, seeking what they do not. *"Nerve and line"* suggests not just a kite, but also a fisherman. The parents are patient as they continue to fly the kite for the child, but they are also afraid for him, as their fragility has been made evident by the events of 9/11. They are acutely aware of what is *"irredeemable"*, something *which cannot be saved*, in the biblical sense, or *paid back* in the monetary sense. There is a suggestion that the parents are aware that they cannot save their child from horror, time or death, and that time itself cannot be recovered or bought.

In his "*The Four Quartets - Burnt Norton*", (a notoriously difficult poem), T. S. Eliot describes time as "*unredeemable*". It is likely that Burnside is referencing Eliot's lines:

Time present and time past
Are both perhaps present in time future
And time future contained in time past.
If all time is eternally present
All time is unredeemable.

An Easy Passage – Julia Copus

This intensely realised poem reads as if the poet is recalling a personal experience. It marks the *"passage"* between childhood and adulthood of a young girl, using her clandestine escapade to the beach with a girl-friend as a *metaphor* for the transition. The *"Easy"* of the title is ironic – the girl makes her return home look *"easy"*, but it is potentially hard and dangerous, just as adolescence can be. The theme **of Growing Up** or **Ageing** is also central to *"To my Nine-Year-Old Self"*, *"Genetics"* and *"Material"*. The poem also comments on **women's position in society**, and could be linked with *"The Gun"* or *"A Minor Role"*.

The poem is in free verse with no regular rhythm or rhyme scheme and comprises only four sentences, the last being twenty-one lines long. It is the choice of line break that gives the poem its structure, each line containing either a single picture or idea, with forward momentum created by the use of *enjambment*. The poem's narrative contains many moments of hesitation, or stillness, followed by movement, and Copus uses the line breaks to mimic the movements of the poem's protagonists and their relationships in both space and time. The use of the extended metaphor of the house can be linked to *"Chainsaw..."*.

The poem starts *in media res*[15] – the perspective of the reader is as a watcher of an incident that is unfolding, but the beginning has already happened before we "arrive on the scene". This has made the poem open to misinterpretation, as the reader tries to sort out the sequence of events and the relationship between the three people in the poem. Copus however, has been very precise in her use of language. The child, or young girl, is climbing back into her house - she is *"half-way **up** there"*, having climbed out

---

[15] *In media res* – in the middle of things

earlier to go to the beach with her friend – *"the friend ...waiting for her...somewhere beneath her."* She is climbing back into the house to then go downstairs and let her friend in. They are in this plight because the mother *"does not trust her daughter with a key"*, effectively imprisoning her in the house. The girl, however, has climbed out, leaving an upstairs window open for her return. The poem starts with the girl crouched on the porch of the house, just prior to making the most difficult part of the return journey, through the open window with its *"narrow windowsill"*. The girl's ingenuity in achieving her freedom shows the futility of trying to inhibit the process of growing up.

Throughout, Copus uses the house as an *extended metaphor* of childhood and the outside world as the domain of adults. For now, she can move between them, through an open window, although not through an open door. She is still controlled by her mother. She has to find a way to open that door for herself. The child has ventured into this adult world through a window, illicitly, defying parental control. As the poem opens, the girl is trapped *"trembling"* between the two. She is *"crouched in her bikini"* on the porch roof. It is an indicator of her position as poised on the verge of adulthood, but not yet ready to make the transition. A bikini is an adult's costume, designed to show off the female body in a way that was considered quite shocking when it was first introduced in the mid-20th century. The girl aspires to adulthood – and yet is acting like a child, and is considered still a child by her mother. The use of *"crouched"* and *"trembling"*, images of fear, suggest that, if this adventure is frightening, then the girl is not ready for the far greater, and more frightening, adventure that is adult life. The most fearful part of this journey back into the safety of the house – symbolic of her retreat back into childhood – is the *"narrow windowsill"* which she has navigated to escape, but now appears more challenging on her return. Notice the use of *enjambment,* between *"narrow windowsill, the sharp/drop of the stairwell"*, to show the contrast between her stillness on the porch roof as she steadies herself for the final move and the danger she faces once she does. The window, however, is *"open"* – not yet beyond her grasp – and the side of the house, against which she will have to press as she reaches for the window-sill, is *personified* as a *"warm flank"*, comforting, like the body of her mother.

Her youth is further evident in her being *"half in love"* with the friend waiting to be let into the house below and on whom she focuses to steady herself for the final part of her journey back. She is not yet sure whether this is "true love" or a "crush", a phase through which young girls often go as they explore their emerging sexuality. However, she is aware of her friend watching her and does not want to fail. The reference to *"petrified beach"* is to the asphalt with which the roof is covered, a type which embeds small pebbles in the bitumen. It is an echo of the beach where these two have been for their adventure, but also a pun. The word *"petrified"* literally means *"turned to stone"* which is what the roof-covering is. However, we take the word to mean *"frightened"*, so it is also being used as a *transferred epithet,* or *Hypallage,* for the feelings of the girl.

As she crouches, the poet draws our attention to her *"tiny breasts"*, at this point in her physical development only just emerging, resting *"lightly"* as she crouches, in contrast to the fullness and weight that will come with maturity. The poet breaks off from her narrative at this point, as if that image, perhaps more than any other, causes her to reflect on the girl's future as a woman. As she is now, the world is open to her; she is unaware of the constraints and restraints that the world will put upon her as an adult woman and how she will be shut out from opportunities. The word *"admit"* refers back to the open window through which the child has come and gone freely, but may be shut to her in adulthood.

For now, both girls are surrounded by their own halo of youth – *"lit as if from within"* – and their friendship; the rest of the world, is shut out as they focus on the house they are about to enter together. Copus uses *enjambment* effectively here to give an image of the street outside as being both colourless and dull, (unlike the girls), and also to suggest it is watching them, perhaps enviously, (*"the long grey/eye of the street"*). This final long sentence draws us away from the girl on the porch-roof to the wider-world of adults – the absent mother, the workers in the dull (*"drab"*) factory across the road and particularly to the *"flush-faced secretary"* who looks up from her magazine just in time to see the final moment of the drama unfolding across the street. The woman is characterised as being one of those whom Copus has exclaimed that the world admits *"less and less"*. She is trapped in a dull job, living in a dream-world where she imagines herself taking evening classes, or taking *"a trip of a lifetime"*, to gain admittance to a wider world, but, instead, looks to the horoscopes in a magazine to passively read about her future, rather than living it. Note how the secretary's reality is brought home by the use of *enjambment* between *"full of the evening class/she plans to take"*. Notice also the way the words *"looks up now"* hang on the end of the line – what does she see? The secretary's thoughts on what she sees, given to us in her own words, indicated by the expressions *"thirteen if she's a day"* and *"next to nothing"*, and perhaps touched by envy (suggested by the emphasis given in positioning it after the enjambment of *"standing/in next to nothing"*), is that the girl below in her bikini is too old to be dressed like that in public, reinforcing her adherence to limiting conventions. It also positions the girls' ages on the division between childhood and adolescence. The secretary's gaze follows that of the waiting girl upwards, to where her friend on the roof has just successfully navigated the narrow window-sill and drops into the house.

As the girl moves, the sunlight picks out the details of her leg and feet, revealing that they are adorned with a *"silver anklet"* and that her toenails are painted. The choice of these details is significant. An *"anklet"* is a modern item of jewellery that has lost its connotations with slavery, from which it originated, and is now rendered light and harmless. However, Copus has chosen it to underpin her views on women's role in society and the limiting of opportunity, of which this girl is as yet unaware. The toenail varnish is similarly harmless; it is not, perhaps, the brave, bright red worn by a full-grown woman, but an almost apologetic, neutral, *"oyster"*. Also, it has probably gone unnoticed by the protective mother; only when it catches the sun is it seen to *"shimmer"* and appear defiant. These adornments will become the girl's *"armaments"* against the adult world, but at the moment, they appear as a mere *"flash"*, rather than the full-blown armour she will need to wear against the challenges facing her in womanhood.

In the imagery of the house as childhood and the outside world as adulthood, there is perhaps another significance in the girl down below waiting to be let in through the now opened door. The protagonist admits to being *"half in love"* with her, unsure, yet aware, of her feelings. The girl below could be considered as a first intrusion of the adult world into the girl's childhood, heralding the imminent transition between the two, through a transfiguring sexual experience.

The Deliverer – Tishani Doshi

This poem uncompromisingly documents the fate of female babies born to poorer sections of Indian society, where infanticide is still practiced. The title *"The Deliverer"* has a number of connotations. A mother delivers a baby; the mother in the poem delivers the child to a third party; a "delivery" is something - letter, parcel - which loses identity whilst it is in transit; the Lord's Prayer asks God to "deliver us from Evil", meaning "save us". In doing so, it explores the nature of **Motherhood,** and **the role of women in society.** In this it links to *"Material"* and in the abuse of women with *"Eat Me"*.

The poem is set out as if it is a newspaper or television report, with the location of the two linked events prefacing each section. The first section is set in a convent in Kerala, India, the second begins in the USA but recalls India at the end. The short lines give a terse, unemotional tone to the whole, like a report, at odds with the subject matter. The story is told by the daughter of the mother who "delivers" the abandoned baby to adoptive parents in the USA. Her tone, although short of being critical of her mother, does suggest a coolness towards her mother's role as "postman", one that is perhaps less emotional and more rational.

The first section opens at a Convent in Kerala, where a nun (*"sister"*) is explaining that the convent rescues babies abandoned by their parents because they are *"crippled or dark or girls"*. The nun's stark explanation shows that the parents of these babies make no distinction between physical disability, cosmetic preference, or gender – all are equally unacceptable to parents probably too poor to be able to support children who cannot work, or are unmarriageable, or are an economic burden. She lists how the babies arrive at the convent, all disposed of like garbage. The victim of the most horrendous treatment has been dug up by a dog, thinking it is a bone. The last line of the section, separated for impact, tells us that this is the child that her mother chooses to bring to adoptive parents in the USA. The use of the word "*one*" strips the child of identity – it is one of many.

The second section opens at the US airport where the adoptive parents await the arrival of their new daughter. The contrast between the eagerly waiting Americans and the callous indifference of the birth parents is described not entirely warmly. "*Ceremony*" sounds somewhat devoid of feeling, having connotations of an act done routinely and unthinkingly, and the positioning of "*tradition*" on the next line may be ironic – America is hardly a byword for "*tradition*", compared, perhaps, to India. Similarly, "*doing things right*" suggests going through motions rather than engaging in the act. The narrator seems to be suggesting that these parents are ignorant of what is to come and the true nature of the "*delivery*" that has been made to them. After all, they are not responsible for what they are sent in the post and may be unprepared for the reality.

This idea is developed in the next stanza, as the narrator reveals that the adoptive parents are ignorant of the obsessive behaviour resulting from the trauma the child has suffered and of the exact circumstances of this child's birth. However, at this moment they are overcome with emotion, as is the narrator's mother: "*We couldn't stop crying*" she says. The adoptive parents cry with the emotion of taking delivery of a child, the mother for delivering to them the child that she has carried as a present from India.

There is some ambiguity in the next stanza. It describes the child as growing up "*on video tapes*" and "*passed from woman to woman*". This could mean that she is left to her own devices and that her parenting is negative in spite of the early enthusiasm. The "*twilight corners*" may mean that she once again retreats to a place where she is unwanted and unloved, as she was when she was born. Alternatively, it could mean that she learns of her early experience through watching "*video tapes*" and that the passing from *"woman to woman"* is a documentary account of how babies like her are rescued from certain death in India. The *"returning"* could mean that these accounts take her imaginatively back to the *"day of her birth"*. Whichever version is preferred, both interpretations allow for the final four stanzas to be a stark commentary on the cyclical nature of the treatment of unwanted children, females in particular, in poor Indian villages. A bleak and graphic account is given of the women leaving their village to secretly give birth, the use of the words *"squeeze"* and *"slither"* suggesting something animalistic, coupled with the dehumanising *"Feel for penis or no penis"*, the casual verb *"toss"* and the visual image of the *"heap of others"*. That this will continue is conveyed by the hopelessness of the word *"trudge"* and the passivity of *"lie down for their men"*, as the women have no choice or agency, and the unwanted babies are disposable. The well-meaning actions of the "mother" and the eager Americans is futile in the face of this institutionalised murder. It will take a revolution in culture and politics to *"deliver"* these unwanted females from misery and death.

The Lammas Hireling – Ian Duhig

Ian Duhig, born in London to Irish parents, is a poet who taps into folklore and myth. In an interview for The Poetry Foundation[16], Duhig recounts hearing the basis for his story from a man in Northern Ireland, who pointed out a witch house where, it was claimed, the dying father turned into a hare. The last thing heard was the *"hare's paws beating the lid of the coffin as they lowered it into the ground."*

In its exploration and use of **myth and legend**, or **the extraordinary,** the poem has similarities with *"Giuseppe"* and *"The Gun"*. These poems are also linked by ideas about **"Othering"** – a fear of those that are different. "Othering", from the point of view of the "othered", can be found in *"Look We Have Coming to Dover!"*

The poem is a *dramatic monologue* written in regular *iambic tetrametre,* but the extensive use of *enjambment* and *caesura,* and the absence of a regular rhyme scheme, give it considerable variation, in keeping with its narrative structure. It is used to effectively create the "voice" of the farmer and to characterise his relationship with the hireling. So, the farmer's self-congratulatory response to getting the hireling cheap is conveyed by the use of the *antithesis*[17] and *enjambment* of *"a light heart/and a heavy purse"* and his ironic comment on his new companion (perhaps in contrast to the dead wife) in the *enjambment* of *"fond of company/that knew when to shut up."* Other *dramatic monologues* in the selection are *"Eat Me"*, *"A Minor Role"*, *"The Gun"* and *"Giuseppe"*.

The title alone points the reader towards a time gone by - both words are likely to be unfamiliar to a modern reader. *Lammas*

---

[16] http://www.poetryarchive.org/
[17] *Antithesis* is a balancing of opposite or contrasting ideas

(from Anglo-Saxon *hlaf-mas* meaning *loaf-mass)* is a pre-Christian festival marking the first grain harvest, held during August. *"Mass"* here means a quantity, not the Christian church ritual. A *Lammas Fair* is held every year in Ballycastle, Co. Antrim, Northern Ireland. A *"Hireling"* is a labourer or worker, often hired for a season to help with the harvest or at lambing. Men would go to "fairs" or markets, as in the poem, and offer their services to farmers who were visiting to sell their animals or produce. A Hireling is someone who only stays for a short time. Ironically, this Hireling stays with the man forever, as a guilty secret which he repeatedly confesses.

The poem opens with a farmer congratulating himself on how cheap the Hireling was. He has made money on what he sold – possibly dairy products as he owns cows – and even after hiring the man as a cow-herd, he has plenty of money left over. He is even more pleased with himself when he finds that the man seems to be some kind of wizard with cows; only female calves - *"heifers"* - are born, which is a bonus, as male calves are useless to a dairy farmer. These cows are healthy and productive, as conveyed by the simile *"fat as cream"* which uses their own product to describe them. The farmer also enjoys the man's company, as he is a good listener. However, this happy state of affairs is not to last. The transition to the next stage of the story is broken across the stanza, to heighten the drama: *"Then one night/disturbed from dreams..."*

In the second stanza, the man awakes from a dream of his wife, to hear what he thinks is her voice, *"torn"* suggesting an unnatural noise or a cry of pain. He finds instead the figure of the hireling, standing naked and caught frozen in the light from his *"dark lantern"* – a kind of candle lantern that enables the light to be shut out completely or give a single beam - with one bleeding foot caught in a fox-trap. Straight away he realises that what he is seeing in front of him is a shape-shifting warlock[18], one who is

41

able to turn into a hare – *"a cow with leather horns"*, referring to the split lip of the hare and its long, brown ears. The epithet is from folklore. The farmer quotes an old saying, meaning that turning into a hare brings much sorrow and much care – it is very unlucky and will end in grief. Again, the saying is split across two stanzas, propelling the story forward.

The farmer does not hesitate in his response - he shoots the man through the heart. As he does so, the moon comes out and by its light, he sees the man transform back into a hare, his skin turning into fur like moss grows on a stone. His skull thins and flattens and his lip draws together in the characteristic split-lip formation of rabbits and hares. His eyes start to protrude like bread rising – rabbits' and hares' eyeballs are prominent and extend beyond the lids. The detailed description of the transformation is obsessive and unsettling.

The farmer carries him in a sack to the river. The *"grew lighter"* is a reference to the man gradually shrinking down to the size of a hare as he transforms. Running water is a traditional ward against the supernatural. The absence of a *"splash"* suggests that the sack's burden is so light that it does not create one – but the end of the story suggests an alternative explanation, as does the story told to Duhig. The bald statement that follows brings us into the present – *"Now"*. The "sting in the tail" of the story is given in sentences that use *enjambment* to keep surprising the reader. The farmer's herd of cows are cursed (*"elf-shot"*). He can no longer sleep and is, in fact, up all night (*"dream/but spend my nights"*) making silver bullets out of his money and his days in the church (*"half-crowns/and my days here"*). Silver bullets are the only way to kill supernatural beings. We realise that the whole poem is a form of confession (*"Bless me Father"*) for his sin of shooting the hare. The final line is chilling in its revelation of the

---

[18] Male witch

extent of his fear of what he has done – he repeats the story as a confession every hour. The silver bullets, taking sanctuary in the church, and confessing his "sin", coupled with the absence of a *"splash"*, suggest that he fears that the warlock may return and exact its revenge.

The feeling of guilt at the end for an action taken against the "other" is echoed in *"Giuseppe"*, where the aquarium keeper, having allowed the killing of the mermaid, cannot look the narrator *"in the eye"*. Both poems explore the irrational fear of difference and how this base instinct results, inevitably and against all reason, in the death of the "othered", even if the "other" has both intrinsic value (for what it is in itself) and extrinsic value (for what it contributes to others). The mermaid is the *"only [one] in the world"* and valuable, the Hireling brings prosperity to the farmer, but even so fear of their difference outweighs their "value". These poems can be seen, perhaps, as having a particular resonance in the current (2016) political climate where fear of the "other" – refugees, immigrants, non-whites - is gaining political traction across the Western world.

To My Nine-Year-Old Self – Helen Dunmore

Helen Dunmore's poem has much in common with "*An Easy Passage*" and "*Genetics*" in its exploration of **Growing-up**, the power of **Memory**, the passage of **Time** and the nature of **Change** as well as the more general theme of **Innocence versus Experience.**

The poem is written in *free verse,* and is conversational as the poet imagines herself talking to her "*nine-year-old self*". Recollections of childhood are interspersed with comments on the effects of aging and the whole is tinged with a rueful, apologetic tone as the poet acknowledges the damage that she has done to her once-youthful body, the awareness of the future and the challenges that await the child, and the older woman's inability to do anything about it. There is a strong evocation of a particular time and place. Dunmore was born in the 1950s and she pinpoints iconic images of those post-war years. These memories suggest that, in spite of the real or imagined danger of the "*men in cars*", childhood then was a time of innocence, when they were left to roam free, away from parental eyes, in a way that is unimaginable to many children today. Memory is made manifest through the "re-incarnation" of her former self by Dunmore.

The poem opens with an apology – the poet is intruding on this child's life, interrupting her going about her childish business, bringing an adult perspective into her world. The idea of the child being surprised and impatient of this intrusion – "*eager to be gone*" – leads to recollections of her youthful self's desire to be always on the move, engaged in physical activity. The "*leap from a height*" also suggests the fearlessness of childhood – children do not "*look before they leap*" as adults do.

The poet ruefully admits that by aging, she has "*spoiled*" their shared body. She contrasts the athleticism of the child with her "carefulness", caused by the aches and pains of aging. At one time, she would spring out of bed and out of the window, eager to be off on an adventure. The older woman's identity momentarily merges with the younger in the use of *"we"*, which replaces the former *"you"*, as she enters imaginatively into her childhood.

The poet recalls the ideas she had, which as a child she would prepare to write down on paper, as, perhaps, she writes her ideas now as a poet, but something more immediately exciting always intruded. The *"bag of sherbet lemons"* anchors the poem firmly in the 50s. In spite of these apparently inconsequential intrusions, she achieved tangible outcomes – a *"factory/trap/den"* – from her imaginings.

In stanza 4, the poet regrets that she cannot, in fact, stay in the past and live off the memory, as time has moved on and she has changed. She allows "herself" to run free, back to her childish adventures. There is some irony in the injunction "[it is] *Time to...*" as, of course, Time is what she does not have. *"Rose-hips"* are the seed pods of wild roses which can be made into jam or jelly, and which she, presumably, picks to sell for tuppence (two pennies in pre-decimal coinage) a pound, thus earning some pocket money. But childhood is not entirely without its dangers and the woman knows that future will not leave this Eden unscathed. Dunmore sounds a darker note with *"scared lanes"*, using *Hypallage,* or a transferred epithet, to describe the places where the girl hides from the *"men in cars"*.

There is incipient danger in the *"lunge"* on a rope over water, the verb suggesting the recklessness of the child's actions. The poet knows, too, that this playground will disappear under houses in the future – but she breaks off from revealing the future, wishing to leave the past untouched and unclouded. The exclamation *"God knows..."* suggests that fear is a constant companion of her older self, aware as she is of the numerous challenges and fears that surround an adult. She leaves her younger self, now firmly separated into "*I*" and "*you*", in a childish, and to adults, disgusting, habit – "*peeling a ripe scab*". The words "*ecstasy*" and "*ripe*" show the child's ability to live in the present moment, with no concept of what the future might bring, including the scars left by experience.

A Minor Role – U A Fanthorpe

U A Fanthorpe is one of the older poets in the selection and died in 2009. For many years, she taught at Cheltenham Ladies College, latterly as Head of English, but in her 40s she abandoned teaching and went to work a s a receptionist in a psychiatric hospital. It was then she started writing poetry, publishing her first volume at the age of 50. Commenting on her late flowering as a poet she said: *"At once I'd found the subject that I'd been looking for all my life: the strangeness of other people, particularly neurological patients, and how it felt to be them, and to use their words."*

Fanthorpe's poem is written in the voice, or voices, of such a subject. It explores mental illness and, in so doing, issues of **Identity.** As they have women as narrators, it can be linked to *"Eat Me"*, and *"Effects"*, which all depict **women who have been marginalised by society.**

The poem is a *dramatic monologue* written in *free verse*, the line lengths seemingly responding to the narrator's thoughts as she recounts her imagined and real experience - at times terse and resigned, at others long and descriptive. The poem is structured by beginning with a metaphor for the persona's *"role"* in life, moving on to a description of visits to a hospital and her life with a mental illness, probably depression, and ending with a return to the opening metaphor and an ironic twist.

Like other poem's in the selection, the title uses a pun. *"A minor role"* is a small part in a play, suggesting that the *persona* lives on the margins of the life being lived by the main parts – the men and women who are unafflicted by her illness and can live full lives. It also suggests that she is playing a part in her real life - that she is hiding the reality of her illness and how it affects her.

The first stanza is a metaphor of the world as a stage; the *"monstrous fabric"* of the penultimate line means a play, as in Shakespeare's *"The Tempest"*: Prospero says *"like the baseless fabric of this vision"* as he dismisses his creation and *"monstrous"* literally means *"full of monsters"*, but also has the modern meaning of *"large"*. She is an unnoticed, marginal character – *spear-carrier, servant* – playing a role that is seemingly insignificant (*"midget moments"*), but should she get it wrong, the whole play (of her life) collapses around her and she is open to ridicule (*"unwanted sniggers"*) from the *"audience"* – the other people in her life.

The second stanza reveals that she would rather not be *"observed"* at all, but stay *"unobtrusive"*. This is in spite of being the patient at the hospital, who should be given centre stage. However, she depicts her "role" there as marginal – driver, parker, comforter. The "Veterans" magazine is published by the Government as an advisory magazine for war veterans, who may be suffering from mental illness such as post-traumatic stress disorder (PTSD). It suggests that while in the waiting room, again someone else takes centre stage. The consultants talk **at** her (*"monologue"*) rather than discuss her condition. She is self-effacing, connects with other *"minor roles"* – the receptionists - and becomes part of the *"background"* to her own life, stoically keeping up appearances.

Stanza 3, with its shorter lines and regular four-stress rhythm, has an increased urgency – she is exposed in the street, *"walking fast"* and wanting to hide. We hear her standard reply: *"getting on, getting better"* to unwelcome, if well-meaning, questions.

Stanza 4 returns to longer lines as she arrives home and contemplates the evening ahead. The attempts to keep the reality of her illness at bay are listed – the desire to escape to bed and oblivion, which *"solves a lot"*, the guarded answering of questions on the phone; the lack of appetite; novels which neither challenge nor disturb; the solace in the cat. She is "play-acting" to herself and the world, pretending to be "normal" by carrying out routine tasks but has to, finally, *"Admit it's not"*.

With this admittance, the depression sets in – *"conjugate"* means to run through all the various forms. Her illness has no outward sign – and this means that cures are difficult. Delays in her treatment are *"ceremonial"*, merely for show, as is the referral to another consultant *"Somewhere else"* (notice the use of *enjambment* here to mimic the move). Even then, she is unimportant, as the Consultant is absent. Nevertheless, she is stoic and resigned, thanking people for every little consideration. There is a tone of bitterness here, as well as resignation, conveyed by the clipped, broken and incomplete sentences.

Her admittance of herself as being *"Not the star part"* is followed by a rhetorical question *"who would want it?"*, as if rejecting the suggestion that she should be treated or viewed as important. Ironically, in being treated like she is: marginalised, unseen, with no voice (except, of course, the one given to her by the poet), she in fact takes on a bigger role. She throws away (*"jettisons"*) the minor roles – *spear-carrier* and *servant*, the tragic chorus which suggests that she would be better off dead, - and declares that by being what she does have a star-part. She is the contrast which makes people who are "normal" see how lucky they are, and how they should live life to the full.

The Gun – Vicki Feaver

In its combination of the **everyday and the mythic,** this poem is similar to *"Giuseppe"* and *"The Lammas Hireling"*. It explores the tension between **Life and Death,** the domestic and sexual **roles of women** and **the links between sexuality and violence.** In the latter, it is similar to *"The Chainsaw and the Pampas Grass"* and *"Eat Me"*.

The poem is in *free verse* and is a *dramatic monologue* spoken by a wife to her husband, who has brought a gun into the house. There is extensive use of *enjambment* to convey the impact of the gun and its victims on the woman, and her growing horror, fascination and sexual arousal.

A gun is, of course, a phallic symbol, as is the chainsaw in Armitage's poem, and this cliché has been explored in the poem to comment on the link between men, violence and sexual potency. As the man uses the gun to kill, and he becomes more "powerful", his physical attraction increases and she becomes *"excited"* and a willing participant in the ritual of death.

The poem opens with a split sentence that states the premise to be explored. There is an immediate contrast made between a gun, with its potential for death, and the house, with its potential for life. What Is *"changed"* by the gun's arrival is the subject of the poem.

The first image of the gun again contrasts the feral and the domestic, the male and the female, spheres. The man lays the gun on the *"kitchen table"*, the centre of the home, around which life revolves. Holding within it the potential to kill, it lies as if a dead animal, as a harbinger of the deaths to come. It is bigger than the table - *"jutting over"* – and casts the *"grey shadow"* of the masculine, and of death, over the cloth, a symbol of the domestic and feminine.

50

The process of "over-shadowing" is gradual – at first harmless fun, shooting at tin cans, the detail of them *"on orange string"* both boyish and silly. However, the violence quickly escalates, with *"the rabbit shot/clean through the head"*, the positioning of the expression over the *enjambment* making a wry comment on whether shooting can ever be *"clean"*.

After the rabbit come so many more victims that her domestic space (the *"fridge"*) is overwhelmed. The use of the continuous past in *"have run and flown"* suggests the on-going and indiscriminate carnage. She is surrounded, now, by the smell of death in the *"gun oil"* on his hands and the animals *"entrails"* – again, the split across the line is designed for contrast and shock. The growing power of the man is conveyed in the use of *enjambment* at *"trample/fur and feathers"* which juxtaposes the violence of the movement with the delicacy of the down-trodden. The man's new -found potency manifests itself in sexual arousal, as when *"sex was fresh"*.

The woman has viewed the gun up until now with a kind of horrified fascination, as she sees it transform her husband from someone who shoots tin cans to someone who sees himself as a conqueror of the weak. However, he is transformed into a sexual predator, as well as animal hunter, and his rediscovered sexual potency excites her, leading to the *paradox* contained in the single line stanza *"A gun brings a house alive"*. They both now feel more *"alive"*.

This *paradox*, of life coming out of death, is continued in the final stanza. She is now complicit in this orgy of death -- sharing in the preparation of the food and cooking it, as if preparing a "feast" for the God that her husband, and she, now worship. This *"black...King of Death"* brings life to them in the symbol of the *"golden crocuses"* appearing in spring. The juxtaposition of *"black"* and *"golden"* and the image of the *"mouth"*, as if giving kisses, is a particularly striking image of this *paradox*.

The Furthest Distances I've Travelled – Leontia Flynn

The poem is written in four, long, loosely structured sentences that trace a woman's realisation about how **Growing Up** and **Time** has changed her perception of the lived life. In this it has links with *"To My Nine-Year-Old Self"* and *"Material"*. It is written in rhyming, or near-rhyming, couplets, sometimes to comic effect, which adds to the ironic tone. The poem, like Dunmore's, is firmly set at a particular time in the poet's life – in this case, the mid 1990s, when Flynn would have been in her early 20s. The opening lines recall her young adult years, and her first, independent travels. Many of the lines are broken and the rhymes awkward, as if to suggest the freedom of her youthful adventures. Towards the end of the poem, the rhymes become more regular and the lines more even in length, as the poet reaches a rueful, if unsettled, maturity.

The opening lines are notably broken and seem determined by the rhyme scheme (*"sack/back, spine/meridian"*) with a humorous gesture toward the rhyme on *"meridian"* as it reflects the theme of travel.

Her exuberance at the freedom of the travelling life is conveyed in the exclaimed *"Yes."* But her "freedom" is in fact quite circumscribed – she is *"on"* not *"off"* the beaten track, following in the footsteps of hundreds of young people before her, and the *"sherpa pass"* again suggests the well-worn. Sherpas are the guides who take people (in increasing numbers) up Mount Everest, on well-known and relatively safe routes. Nor are post-Soviet Zagreb and Krakow particularly adventurous; even the reference to Siberia, a notoriously harsh environment, is undercut by the *enjambment* that links it to *"white/cells of scattered airports"*. So, the older woman is infusing her youthful recollections with irony born of her mature knowledge – the free life she thought she was leading was, in fact, quite tame.

The airport imagery is used to comic effect in the third stanza where she hears, in the voice of the *"tannoy"*, a message that the life she is living is the one she is destined to lead, as if she has heard the word of a 20th century God. The humour also lies in the forced line break at *"anony/mity"* which gives a *half-rhyme* with both *"tannoy"* and *"destiny"*, laughing at the naivety of her younger self.

In the third stanza, she tries, but fails, to account for how her youthful travels have given way to a more mundane adulthood. She attributes it to, maybe, fear of the side-effects of an anti-Malarial drug, (*Lariam* not *"Larium"* as here) which were given press prominence in the early 2000s. Whatever the reason, she now finds that she has exchanged a life in which she lived hand-to-mouth while travelling, using Western Union money exchanges to get funds, for one where she goes to a post-office with bills or unemployment benefit; she has exchanged hastily packing the bare necessities into a *"holdall"* and catching a Greyhound bus to travel the length and breadth of America, for a life of doing the washing. Travel, and the freedom it represented, has been swapped for mundane adult chores and necessities.

The final sentence, running over the last three stanzas, reflects on what she has learned. Her life is still unsettled – *"routine evictions"* suggest that she has not yet settled down into regular domesticity, as do the visits to the laundry and the *"giro"*. However, in clearing out, ready to move on, she finds *"souvenirs"* of the lovers that she has met along her life's journey – small tokens of affection mixed up with abandoned socks and pants - which are her *"valentines"*.

These *"valentines"* are *"alien"*, *"unravelled"* and *"crushed"*, suggesting separation and broken relationships. Her emotional journey, away from the lives of these lovers, has been greater than any physical journey, and all that she has left of these chance encounters are these pathetic *"souvenirs"* of the time she spent with them – not seriously, perhaps, but as a break from daily life.

This reflection on the false promises of travel and the unsatisfactory relationships of youth, may seem pessimistic, were it not for the humorous, self-mocking tone of the poem. Also, Leontia Flynn is one of the youngest poets in the selection and these experiences are those of a young woman with her life still ahead of her.

Giuseppe – Roderick Ford

It is worth a visit to Roderick Ford's website (http://roderickford.com/) as it is visually intriguing and gives some insight to the poem. Ford has Asperger's syndrome, a form of autism, which may be experienced as feelings of alienation or difficulty communicating. The Forward Arts Foundation (which sponsors the poetry prize from which the *"Poems of the Decade"* are selected) comments: "[Ford] *populates his work with solitary, outsider figures, sometimes only partly human, stranded on the borders between worlds and excluded from normal human relationships.*[19]"

"Giuseppe" explores how difference is both marginalised and exploited, and how its intrinsic "value" is made subservient to the needs of the mass, who are seen as the "norm". There are, of course, many examples from history of how this mind-set leads to the sacrifice of individuals and to genocide, and it is difficult to conceive of this poem not being a reference to the attempted extermination of the Jews, and other minorities, during the Second World War. There is criticism of the Catholic Church's response to this genocide, which could be described as "equivocal", in the priest's arguments for killing the mermaid. There is also a strong suggestion that it refers to Christ's sacrifice for Man, perhaps in contrast. The process of "**Othering**" minorities is also the subject of *"The Lammas Hireling"*, *"Effects"*, and *"Look We Have Coming to Dover"*. Another thematic concern is **Guilt**, which is also experienced by the narrators in *"Effects"*, and *"The Lammas Hireling"*, as they recognise the inadequacy of their response to the tragedies enacted before them. Like *"Out of the Bag"* and *"Eat Me"*, it uses images of **Myth and Religion.**

---

[19] http://www.forwardartsfoundation.org/poet/roderick-ford/

The poem is in the form of a narrative in which the narrator recounts a story told to him by his Uncle Giuseppe. The voice of the Uncle is heard in the last line, but this tells us much about the theme of the poem. The story is recounted in flat, regular three and four beat lines, in contrast to the traumatic events recalled, making the whole more chilling in its lack of emotional engagement. This is the voice of the "rational mind", over the rich, chaotic variability of humanity – the voice of fascist regimes everywhere.

Sicily is an island off the coast of Italy much associated with mermaid legends. In particular, Ovid's *"Metamorphoses"* recounts the tale of Acis and Galatea. Galatea was a sea-nymph – one of the 50 Nereids of Roman mythology – who fell in love with the mortal Acis. The cyclops (one-eyed giant) Polyphemus kills Acis with a boulder in a jealous rage. Galatea turns Acis into the Sicilian river Acis so that she and he can join together eternally as he enters the sea. The Allied forces (Britain, America) invaded Sicily in "Operation Husky" in 1943 as part of the campaign to take Italy, at the time a fascist regime allied to Germany, out of the war. In occupied territories elsewhere in Europe, civilians suffering food shortages took to eating zoo animals, a practice to which the poem refers.

"Giuseppe" is the Italian form of Joseph. This should immediately alert us to a religious sub-text in the story recounted. The killing of the mermaid takes place *"behind the aquarium"*, out of sight of the public, already suggesting that the perpetrators are aware of the dubious legitimacy of their actions. *"Bougainvillea"* is a bright red/pink flowering climbing vine, the lushness contrasted with the barren ground on which the mermaid is *"butchered"*. The word equates her with an animal - it is what we do to turn animals into meat. Her uniqueness is clear – she is the *"only captive mermaid in the world"* but even so this does not save her. There are witnesses to her killing – *"a doctor, a fishmonger, and certain*

others". These are the "false witnesses" of the Bible who were brought to bear witness against Christ before his crucifixion. The doctor and the priest declare her to be a fish, while the fishmonger serves her up to the troops.

In the second stanza, the confusion of the Uncle is sustained with the use of *"She, it"*. He is aware of the choices being presented to them – to declare her an *"It"* legitimises the action taken, the *"She"* makes it a mortal sin. The rational approach is to declare that she cannot be human because she has never learnt to speak - language being the ability that distinguishes humans most clearly from animals. However, from a humane viewpoint, she is *"simple"* – human but unable to learn – and from the self-serving viewpoint, not human, and therefore unable to learn. The priest relies on the righteous classifications of the Church to justify his complicity. He holds her hand, to give the last rites, but confirms she is a fish – non-human – and therefore cannot learn to speak. But those who hear her know (although they will not admit it to themselves) that the sounds she makes, although not speech, convey all the anguish of a (human) *"woman in terrible fear"*.

Further confusing evidence is presented to them during the butchering. They take from her a *"ripe golden roe"* – a further equivocal image. The roe is at once her children and fish eggs, giving the "witnesses" further opportunity to justify their actions. This image is also one of the few sensual images in the poem – directing us towards the narrator's perspective perhaps. It is also the final hope for her species, which makes their decision even more morally dubious. Although the doctor declares that *"an egg is not a child"*, he refuses to eat any. He doubts his own judgement and feels guilty. Sicily is a Catholic country and there is a further irony as his argument is also central to Catholicism's rejection of abortion

The cutting off of the head and hands are superstitious rights to ward off evil spirits and prevent the dead returning – as in vampire legends – indicating that they are uncomfortable about their actions. The *"wedding ring"* is a symbol that she is married – and therefore human, as "marriage" is again a unique, human attribute, meaning that the *"golden roe"* was indeed her children and bore the future of the species within it. The feeling of guilt amongst the "false witnesses" grows, as they stop the removal of the ring. This incident most brings to mind the Holocaust, where the wedding rings of the Jews were removed.

The mermaid is cooked and eaten, the men explaining away the feast as a lucky find on the beach, thus compounding their guilt. The uncle tries to justify his actions, by saying that the men were *"starving"*, thus putting the needs of the many above the needs of the one. The reveal of the Uncle being the aquarium keeper, and thus the man who should have saved his prize exhibit, is delayed up to this point, to give his story, and his action, greater impact. The extent of his guilty feeling is conveyed in him being unable to look his nephew, the narrator, in the eye as he tells his story, and the appalled reaction of the nephew is clear from the exclamation *"I thank God"*, as he grapples to come to terms with the enormity of what he has just been told and his uncle's complicity in it.

Out of the Bag – Seamus Heaney

Heaney was born in County Derry, Northern Ireland, to a Catholic family and was the eldest of nine children, one of whom was killed at the age of four in a car-accident. His father and grandfather were farmers and a recurring theme in Heaney's poetry (although not here) is his awareness, and guilt, that he did not follow in his father's footsteps but became a poet and academic. He attended Queen's University, Belfast, but spent the latter part of his life in Dublin. He is certainly the heavy-weight hitter in this collection, one of the finest poets of the 20th century, Nobel Laureate, Oxford Professor of Poetry and winner, in 2006, of the TS Eliot poetry prize.

The poem explores the power of **Imagination**, and how it can create an alternate reality, as in *"History"* and **Memory** and the **relationship between children and parents** and the ties that bind them together, as in *"Material"*. It also creates a strong sense of **Place**, as in *"History"* and examines the overlap between **Myth and Religion**, as in *"Giuseppe"* and *"The Lammas Hireling"*.

The poem is in *tercets* of *iambic pentametre* - five *iambic* beats (ti-**TUM**; light - **HEAVY**) in each line, as indicated here:

And **by** the **time** he'd **reappear** to **wash**

Heaney is a master of the use of *enjambment*. The use of *enjambment* within this regular rhythm maintains the flow between lines, and particularly across the *tercets,* varying the emphasis for effect as he points up images and ideas:

And **by** the **time** he'd **reappear** to **wash**

Those **no**sy, **ro**sy, **big**, soft **hands** of **his**
In the **scu**llery **ba**sin,

One of Heaney's favourite tricks is to use *enjambment* and *caesura* (a break in the middle of the line) to create an emphasis on key words, by putting them at the beginning of the line following the *enjambment*, and inverting the light-**heavy** beat (*iamb*) and using a **heavy** - light beat (**TUM**-ti – a *trochee*), to mimic the meaning of the words themselves:

> **Then** *like a* **hyp***notist*
> *Un***win***ding* **us***, he'd* **wind** *the* **instru***ments*

> **Back** *in***to** *their* **lin***ing,*

or

> *The* **ba***by* **bits** *all* **came** *to***ge***ther* **swim***ming*

> *In***to** *his* **soa***py* **big** *hy***gie***nic* **hands**

All this gives his poems a sense of being thoughtful, musing recollections, deceptively casual, as if the poetry emerges out of reminiscence, but it is always guiding us to his meaning.

Heaney is recalling, partly from a child's perspective, the birth of his younger siblings. The central conceit is that the babies have come out of Dr Kerlin's bag, just as his instruments do, when the doctor attends the regular confinements of Heaney's mother. Home births would have been the norm during Heaney's childhood – routine hospitalisation for birth is a late 20th century phenomena. The poem is in four distinct parts – **part I** describes the Doctor and his delivery of the baby, as if it were a mysterious rite; **part II** takes us to Epidaurus in Greece where he muses on the origins of medicine and its rites, and, as in Lourdes where he made a pilgrimage one summer, he almost faints from the heat and has a hallucinatory vision of the Doctor; **part III** sees him re-enacting an ancient ritual of sending an item from the shrine to the sick; **part IV** returns to his childhood memories of the births.

1

The focus of the first part is Doctor Kerlin, seen through the eyes of Heaney as a child, but with the adult's wry perspective on the rites the Doctor performs, which seemed to him so mysterious at the time. For the child, the Doctor's medical bag – a large, leather, "Gladstone" bag which every doctor carried when they made home visits – is like a magician's hat out of which the Doctor pulls his *"instruments"* but also the babies. Notice the use of *euphemism* in the word *"room"*. The child is not sure what is happening; the births are shrouded in mystery; *"the room"* (his parents' bedroom) becomes a mysterious, sacred place – an *"inner sanctum"* as in a temple where rites are performed.

Heaney uses highly sensual imagery to describe the Doctor's ritual washing of his hands after the birth. The *internal rhyme* (*nosy, rosy*) focuses on the parts of the Doctor most relevant to his task. *"Nosy"* suggests that his hands have been where they should not – an adult Heaney joke. The bag is an integral part of the Doctor – he is never seen by the child without it. Its soft, worn, leather inside reminds him of the inside of a dog's ear. Later, it is described as an "Ark", (*"ark by the keel"*) not just Noah's ark, but also a storage space for holy relics – as in "Ark of the Covenant". The "magic" of the bag is captured in the phrase *"empty for all to see"*, recalling the actions of magicians after they perform a trick. The bag is empty once the birth is over as he has used the instruments to deliver the baby. The child is fascinated. The taking out of instruments (like the taking out of the child from the uterus) seems to happening in reverse as the instruments are put back in place in the bag.

The Doctor makes frequent visits to the family, as it was a large one, and Heaney continues to paint a vivid picture of his impact on the child. The *"Dutch interior gleam"* is a reference to paintings by 17th century painters, such as Vermeer, who painted domestic scenes and were notable for their depiction of light. Heaney describes the ritual of preparing the hot water for him after the birth. The water is prepared to just the right temperature – not so hot as to swell his hands (*"plumping"*) but gentle and full of soapsuds. *"Sud-luscious"* is a *neologism*[20], created by Heaney, perhaps as a child who was even then inventive with language. The water used is reserved for this purpose - it comes from the *"rain-butt"*, because rain water lacks calcium and therefore produces a better lather.

The Doctor is brisk and matter-of-fact in his work, conveyed by the adverbs *"hard and fast"*, and *"suddenly"* as he prepares to leave. At this point in the ritual, for once, he looks at the "invisible" child watching him and in his cold, blue eyes, the child sees even greater mysteries – and not a little horror.
Hyperborean is Greek for a people who lived "beyond the North Wind" - suggesting the doctor is other-worldly, a mythical person. The child looks through the *"peep-holes"* of the Doctor's eyes to imagine the room he works in, like some kind of Frankenstein laboratory where he creates babies out of parts, a chamber of horrors.

These last four tercets show Heaney's masterful use of language to create unforgettable images. Look at the use of the vowels *i* and consonant *l* in these lines, followed by the use of *o* and *oo* and then the final resolution in *ol*:

skimmed
Milk and ice, swabbed porcelain, the white

And chill of tiles, steel hooks, chrome surgery tools
And blood dreeps, in the sawdust where it thickened
At the foot of each cold wall.

This is painting with words - quite literally - as he moves from the sterility of the imagined laboratory (**i** and **l**) to the awful vision of the blood which must accompany his "baby making" (**o** and **oo**),

---

[20] A *neologism* is a newly invented word

coming together as it "*dreeps*" – drips and seeps - down the "**cold**" walls. Genius.

The laboratory seems to be mixed up with the scullery in the child's mind, the hooks probably recalling the hooks in the ceiling from which farmers would hang meat or bacon. In the child's imagination, there are baby-parts hanging from them. The final line is both humorous and awful, as Heaney likens the end of a tiny penis hanging from the line to the rosebud in the Doctor's buttonhole, thus identifying him as the creator of the "monsters".

2

This part of the poem is challenging, as it expects the reader to know a number of literary, historical and religious references. It is written from the perspective of the adult Heaney, on a visit to Epidaurus, where he reflects on the origins of medicine in Ancient Greece and the place of ritual in its practice. Epidaurus is a major Greek archaeological site in northern Greece and the town was dedicated to Asclepius, the Ancient Greek God of Healing. The "*rod of Asclepius*" was a snake-entwined staff, which remains the symbol of doctors today. "*Poeta doctus*" means a learned poet who refers to the classics, and Heaney has given the title to the poet/writer Peter Levi. Levi wrote extensively on Greece and Heaney is referring to his studies. The shrines of Asclepius became places where people would go to be cured – rather as, in the Christian religion, pilgrimages are made to Our Lady of Lourdes in France, as documented by Robert Graves, another scholar-poet. Playing on the idea, of "poet" and "doctor", Heaney believes his own power to heal comes from Poetry ("*poeta*" rather than "*doctus*"), a power that comes unbidden – an "*epiphany*". Poetry was often considered to be divinely inspired. Heaney sees that the "*whole place*" is not simply a shrine to the God of Healing, but a system of facilities designed to aid the healing process. The idea of "*incubation*", as described, is similar to the Native-American ritual of the "sweat lodge", a ceremony which could similarly end with the revelation of a god.

"*Incubation*" is also a word used for the period between laying and hatching eggs – another reference to birth.

Heaney walks around this sacred site in hot sun, "*Hatless, groggy*", as he did back in Lourdes some years earlier, on a pilgrimage with the Derry Diocese (in 1956 Heaney would have been 16). On that pilgrimage, he acted as a "*thurifer*", the boy who carried the incense-burner swung before processions in Catholic rituals. The "*heat and fumes*" made him feel faint, in much the same way he feels faint, now, in Epidaurus. As he bends to pick some grass (why becomes evident in Part 3), he has his own "*epiphany*" or hallucination. He imagines Dr Kerlin drawing the kinds of pictures of men and women that children do, in the steam on the scullery window, "*creating*" people on the window pane. He envisions the Doctor carrying out his ritual washing and – a miracle! The pieces of baby that were previously imagined as hanging from hooks now "*come together*" as he performs his sacred rites. Like one emerging from a trance-like state, Heaney recovers, "*blinking and shaky*" into the sunlight.

3

Heaney has pulled up the "*bits of grass*" as another ritual. He sends off the bits of grass to people who are sick – as visitors to shrines would do in ancient times. He is reluctant to meet up with other people; he wants to feel the spirit of the place by lying on the ground and hoping that he will be visited by *Hygeia*, (from where we get the word "hygiene"), Asclepius's daughter, who gave continuing good health. The "*undarkening door*" suggests that she keeps away death.

4

Heaney returns to his childhood recollections of the births of his siblings, the fantasy he created as a child as real to him now as then - the memory has been retained clearly over the time that has elapsed. He is allowed into "*The room*" after the Doctor has left, where he sees his mother lying on the bed. He knows (now) that the sheets on the bed have been put on specially for the birth. Wedding present sheets were kept for "best" in many working-class households, as they were often higher quality than those bought for everyday use, and kept for special occasions, as they were irreplaceable. This is another example of Heaney's evocation of a particular place and time. Heaney refers back to his vision at Epidaurus. "*Incubating for real*" can mean either, or both, that Heaney is creating this poem (Heaney, looking back, sees that this was the inspiration for the poem) or the child is awaiting the revelation of where these babies really come from. The child peers at, and appears to, his mother as she slips in and out of sleep. She smiles at him; her glance is described as a "*precinct*" – the entrance to a temple. This is a ritual they go through for every birth, the mother asking the same question and in so doing, maintaining the mystery of the births. Heaney, when a child, is denied his "*epiphany*".

Like "*To My Nine-Year-Old Self*", much of the effectiveness of this poem, and the humour, comes from the dual perspectives of the child and the adult that are presented in the first and final parts. Heaney allows us in on the "joke" of the child's misconception of the nature of his siblings' births, whilst conveying the child's wonder and horror at the contents of Dr Kerlin's bag.

Effects – Alan Jenkins

This is another poem with a title which has a variety of meanings, like *"Material"*, *"An Easy Passage"* and *"The Deliverer"*. *"Effects"* here means: *"personal effects"*, the things the mother leaves behind when she dies; the impact of the death on the son; the impact of the death of the husband and father on the mother. Like *"Material"*, *"Genetics"*, *"The Deliverer"* *"On Her Blindness"* and *"Out of the Bag"*, the narrator is an adult child reflecting on his or her **relationship with a parent**, in which he or she recounts an intensely realised personal experience. It also explores feelings of **Guilt**, as in *"Giuseppe"*, *"The Gun"* and *"To My Nine-Year-Old Self"*. The poem also explores **Identity** and, like *"Out of the Bag"*, and *"To My Nine Year Old Self"* it recalls a particular time – the mid-20th century of the poet's childhood.

This autobiographical poem is an *elegy*, written in two, long sentences, with considerable subordination, which enables Jenkins to move between the past and the present and delay, until the last few lines, the revelation that he arrived too late to see his mother before she died. The poem opens with the son holding the dead woman's hand; the bulk of the poem recounts the last years of his mother's life, after the death of his father, through the device of the missing rings and watch, which are part of her identity. The poem reaches an uneasy resolution when these items are brought to him by the *"nurse"* in a *"little bag"*. Although written in free verse, the line lengths are relatively equal in length and considerable use is made of rhyme, which gives the whole a feeling of contained emotion as the son tries to come to terms with his relationship with his mother – and his feelings of guilt. In fact, control and non-disclosure characterise this poem as a whole and may reflect the relationship between mother and son.

The hand the son holds bears the marks of her life; he holds it as if reading a palm, not to tell the future, but to illuminate and describe her past. It is the hand of a woman who has worked hard, much of it in the service of husband and son. They are active hands – *"chopping, slicing/scrubbing"*. The focus is on her cooking, *"giving love the only way she knew"* suggesting that she was not a woman given to displays of affection and that this may have impacted his relationship with her as he grew to adulthood. This is supported by the disconnect of *"she cooked and we ate"* – even the food seems unable to bridge a divide between them. The rhymes on *"scarred/hard, plate/ate, knew/stew"* add to the immediacy of the description, bringing the woman vividly to life.

As he holds her hand, he notices that her rings are missing, which leads to further reminiscence on her life as a wife. The *"they"* gives us a clue as to the circumstances which the poet is recalling – but without, again, giving much away. We might assume that she is in a hospital or nursing home at this point. These rings had been kept in a drawer, all but forgotten, along with items from a by-gone era (*"tortoiseshell combs"*) and souvenirs of her past, including snapshots of family holidays taken *"abroad"*, at a time when going *"abroad"* was a rare event. The italics seem to suggest that the son views his parents concept of *"abroad"* as somewhat quaint. However, on the death of her husband, the rings are brought out and worn. The son makes a wry, and perhaps unkind, or merely uncomprehending, comment on this – that she showed that she was married only after her husband was dead. Whether this is resentment on the part of the son, or indicative of a troubled marriage, is unclear. However, a more charitable explanation would be that wedding and engagement rings are precious, and easily lost by a woman who clearly spent much of her time *"chopping, slicing, scrubbing"* on behalf of her men-folk.

He also notices that her watch has gone. The symbolism is evident – time no longer matters to this woman. However, the watch also gives another window into her life, and perhaps his relationship with her, or his feelings about the life she led. It is a *"Classic ladies' model, gold strap"*; the *hyphenated* description is perfunctory, almost dismissive, as if the ordinariness of the watch is a comment on her conventionality, which he despises. The watch is something she always wore; again, the italicised *"that"* seems a criticism. He recalls his mothers' and fathers' lives together – sitting on the sofa watching programmes on the television that he refuses to watch (*"disdained"*) because they were beneath him.

The poet now reveals, abruptly, that their roles as carer and cared for has, at some point, reversed – it is he who cooks for her. He cooks her the kinds of meals that she used to cook for him – and again, there is a tone of condescension in the description of this food as *"English, bland"* and her dismissal of *"funny foreign stuff"*, which characterises both her age and the post-war era in which he grew up. She continues to wear the watch throughout the period that she descends into the loneliness of widowhood, possible alcoholism and depression, and eventually into a psychiatric ward. During this decline, there are weeks when he *"doesn't come"* to see her, imagining her watching the *"snow"* on television after the programming has ended, drinking heavily her dead husband's whiskey *"to be with him again"*. The time in the psychiatric ward slowly strips her of her mind and her identity, as she lives in the past, and draws from him the admittance that as he grew up he *"learned contempt"* for her world. Even as she becomes mentally and physically weaker, she shows some pride – distinguishing herself from the *"poor souls"* who seem to have lost all awareness of self, even though she is drugged and unresponsive.

The "*But now…*" brings us to the present, and back to the beginning of the poem, where he sits holding her dead hand, empty of rings, with a "*thick rubber band*" in place of the ubiquitous watch, signifying the final stripping of identity from her. The hands that he remembered and described in such detail at the beginning as strong and active, are now "*blotched and crinkled*" and motionless, unable to make even the feeble gestures urging her son to stay with her that she made on his last visit, and ignored, just as he ignored what he now knows to have been her last words: "*Please don't leave*". He has returned, but too late for her to know that he is there. Thankfully, she is also unable to see the signifiers of her identity, from which she has been separated in death – the watch and the rings – brought to him by the nurse in the "*little bag*" to which her life has been reduced.

The poet's reaction to his mother's death is, arguably, ambiguous. There are clear indications in the language of the opening that there was a distance between his mother and him, and possibly between his parents. He admits his "*disdain*" for his parents' life, at least when he was an adolescent, or perhaps he shows incomprehension of the norms of an earlier era. At times, he is dismissive of their small pleasures and their life-style. He also reveals his long absences during her widowhood, leaving her to drink alone "*Night after night*", and seems to acknowledge that her dreams, when she has slipped into depression and either senility, or a drug-induced haze, were of her own childhood and a time "*before/[he] was born*", suggesting that these were possibly happier. Maybe she was more aware of his "*learned contempt*" than he admits to himself. The tone seems to be less one of guilt than a matter-of-fact acknowledgement that he could have been a better son. This ambiguity in tone may reflect what one commentator has described as Jenkins' "*stylised confessionalism*".

Genetics – Sinead Morrissey

Central to this poem is the childhood finger rhyme, of which a number of versions exist. Here is the version I learned as a child in the 1950s, with a little prompting from the web on the second verse!

Here's the Church and here's the steeple
Look inside* and there's the people.
Here's the parson, going upstairs.
Listen to his daily prayers:

"Dearly beloved brethren, isn't is a sin
To eat all the potatoes and throw away the skin?
The pigs eat the skin, the pigs feed us
Dearly beloved brethren, what a load of fuss!"

*sometimes *"Open the door"*

There are illustrations and descriptions on the internet – most of them of dubious authenticity. The first YouTube video presented has the correct finger movements – but the man in the creepy mask is terrifying! https://www.youtube.com/watch?v=erAy-F-V0LA.

Morrissey's poem dwells on the nature of our genetic inheritance, the ties that bind us to our parents even if they are physically absent. It has a tone of wistful regret, as she dwells on the absent father and her feelings of abandonment, her genetic inheritance bringing some kind of solace. It is thematically linked to a number of other poems in the selection – *"Material"*, *"Effects"* and *"On Her Blindness"* – in the exploration of **relationships between parents and children.** It also explores ideas about **Identity.**
The poem is broadly in the form of a *villanelle,* a highly-structured verse form comprising 19 lines – five stanzas of *tercets* and a final

quatrain – and using only three rhymes. In a pure *villanelle*, the first and third lines are also repeated with strict regularity, but in this poem, they are used more as echoes of each other. Morrissey also uses *half-rhyme* to sustain the rhyme. Even so, she creates a tightly woven poem, just as the strands of our DNA are structured around the double-helix.

The first *tercet* considers how our physical characteristics are a product of the mixing of the genes of our parents, using her hands as a conceit for the mixing of the two parents' genetic material. Of course, she cannot see the various genes of her parents in her hands – they are both indivisible and invisible. Holding up her hands reassures her that she had two parents and this gives her a strong sense of self and identity. The triple rhyme scheme is set up in *"palms/pleasure/hands"*, although it will be varied., just as no one person is a carbon copy of their parents.[21]

The second stanza reveals that the parents have separated, perhaps not amicably, as the word *"repelled"* suggests animosity. She is comforted in that even though they are apart and leading new lives, they still come together in her hands. The poet uses the *full* and *half-rhymes "lands/hands, pleasure/lover, palms/palms"*, to link to the first *tercet*.

In the third stanza, she considers the implications of the separation on others – the mutual friends of the married couple, who now hunt (*"quarry"*) through memories, or photos, perhaps, of the couple being together. However, she is able to find evidence of their union, at any time, by looking at her hands.

The idea of *"marriage"* leads, in the fourth and fifth stanzas, to the childhood game, where a "church" is formed by interlocking

---

[21] Thanks to *Ella* of the AS English blog for this observation
https://blogasenglish.wordpress.com/

the fingers and pointing the forefingers upwards to form the "steeple". By turning the interlocked fingers over, you can see the "people" inside the church (the fingers). In this, she sees her two parents standing together once more as they did at the altar on their marriage day. The game "re-enacts" their marriage and further evidence of their union is in her body – the *"register"*, or formal record, of their marriage.

The *quatrain* is addressed to a lover or husband, urging him to follow the genetic imperative to reproduce and have a child with her. As her parents *"made"* her a *"mirror"* of them, so their child will be a combination of the two of them. In the last line, there may be a pun on *"made by hand"*, as in "not by machines", as this reproduction is natural and non-mechanistic, each individual being unique, a "one-off". In its address to a lover, she puts the ghost of her parents behind her and looks to the future with another.

From the Journal of a Disappointed Man – Andrew Motion

Andrew Motion is the former Poet Laureate. It would be fair to say that he has never achieved the popular, or maybe literary, appeal of Ted Hughes, whom he succeeded in 1999, nor of Carol Ann Duffy, who took over the role in 2009. He himself described being Poet Laureate as *"difficult"* and "*very, very damaging to [his] work*[22]". He has not been widely anthologised as part of the Exam syllabus, as have the other two.

"Journals" (literally *"daily"*, like *"diary"*) were originally records of events in a person's life with reflections on their reactions to it, written for private consumption, but often with a view to later publication. The title is probably taken from the Journal of the same name written by "Wilhelm Nero Pilate Barbellion" (1889 – 1919), the *nom-de-plume* of Bruce Frederick Cummings, who died of multiple sclerosis, aged 30, and which has become a minor literary classic. *"Disappointed"* is a euphemism for a life cut tragically short by a disease of which Barbellion himself was unaware until he was 26 and had less than five years to live. His life was left unresolved. Certainly, the subject matter of the poem seems more *ego-centric*, more concerned with the poet's private reaction to an event, rather than a reflection on his relationship with parents, lovers or children, which characterises the bulk of the selection.

The challenge of the wooden pile can be seen as a metaphor for the challenge of finding meaning in, or the meaning of, Life. Faced with **bringing meaning to Life**, even strong men, who seem to know what they are doing, fail to resolve the challenge, in spite of struggling manfully. All the writer can do is look on helplessly,

---

[22] *BBC News Online. 10 September 2008*

his words useless. He is left with a realisation, perhaps, that all we can do is keep trying, or simply give up. This theme runs through *"History"*, *"Ode to a GP Urn"*, and *"A Minor Role"* and occurs also in *"Effects"* and *"On Her Blindness"*.

The poem is written in free verse, but with regular line lengths. Together with the matter-of-fact tone created by the use of colloquialisms and the lack of poetic embellishment, this gives us the sense of reading a factual *"account"* of the incident. The poet seems remarkably detached from the men who are the subject of his observation and from the activity in front of him. The language, although straightforward, seems stiff and formal, although he *"talks"* a lot, in contrast to the mono-syllabic and sparse utterances of the workmen. The poet is well aware of his separation from the men – physically and linguistically– but is also frustrated that he cannot do anything to help them. In spite of his *"superior"* language, product of a different social-economic standing and education, he is yet helpless in the situation unfolding in front of him. This leads to his *"disappointment"* – his inability to enter imaginatively into their world, to work together perhaps, and the lack of a satisfactory resolution to the puzzle presented.

The air of detachment is immediate from the first stanza. He *"discovers these men"* as if by accident, *"these"* emphasising their difference from him, and their anonymity. He describes the equipment they use as *"paraphernalia"* – an indistinguishable pile of *"stuff"*, which he then lists indiscriminately, showing his lack of familiarity with their world of work. That they are skilled, however, is evident in the emphasis on *"massive"* and the latent danger in this *"massiveness"* swinging over them – as suggested by splitting the enjambment of *"swinging"* and *"over"* across the first and second stanza.

74

Not only is the *"wooden pile"* (usually a whole tree-trunk cut to form a vertical support) massive, but its size is mirrored by the workmen, depicted as other-worldly (from him) beings – *"powerful/ruminative/silent/ignoring"*) which emphasises the poet's insignificance and their strength.

Unlike the poet, to whom words are "tools", the men are not interested in verbalising their dilemma or reflecting on it. They are concerned with practical matters, giving a series of commands to each other in *"monosyllables"* – unlike the poet's use of long words. The poet has to learn their language to understand what is happening in front of him - the *"obscure movements"* which show him that they are being presented with a difficult challenge.

However, in deciphering the action in front of him he is only partially successful. He needs someone to explain it to him in words, his natural, or learned, medium. But the men, described as *"monsters"*, again emphasising the gulf between them, are *"silent"* and so he initially misreads the reason. They are not confused by the challenge in front of them, but *"tired"*, tired of the task and of the constant challenges presented to them – tired, in fact, of *"the whole business"* of life. This idea is developed in the reference to *"crack of Doom"*, which means eternity. In spite of their strength, these men are being worn down by life and although they do not give up without a struggle, they are ultimately beaten.

The men, having given up on the challenge facing them, seek enlightenment in gazing into the water, like "mystics" or religious believers, searching for answers. One even makes a kind of "offering" of his spit, his *"round eyes"* suggesting wonderment, as he watches it disappear into the sea. But he receives no answer.

The figure of the foreman, leader, *"most original thinker"*, and this most likely to come up with answer to the puzzle, is similarly baffled. He has tried all sorts of solutions but none have worked. His resignation is evident in smoking a cigarette – signal that the work is over and that they can "knock off". His authority, and air of finality, is given in his *"heavy kind of majesty"*.

The men know when they are beaten and waste no more time on it, abandoning the project and walking away. They do not indulge in futile efforts. The poet, however, is left behind – with the problem or question still unresolved and a feeling of disappointment that no solution to the puzzle has been found.

Like *"The Furthest Distances…"*, the poem ends without a satisfactory resolution. There is experience and some learning, but the way forward is less clear. However, whilst Flynn's poem is written with some humour and a sense of her writing about a passing stage in her life, Motion's poem has a weightiness which perhaps reflects the "disappointment" of a much older man approaching late life and searching for answers.

Look We Have Coming to Dover – Daljit Nagra

Daljit Nagra is a poet who uses the distinctive dialect of Indians whose first language is Punjabi (sometimes called *"Punglish"*), to affectionately characterise their experience of living in Britain, often with comic effect. He is himself a first-generation, English-born Sikh whose parents came to Britain in the late 1950s. The poem, published in 2004, is included in his debut collection of poems, which has the same title, and which won the 2007 Forward prize.

The poem's title is written in *"Punglish"* and it, and the dedication, references the 19th Century poet Matthew Arnold's poem *"Dover Beach"* and probably WH Auden's *"Look, Stranger"*. It also alludes to the 1967 film about inter-racial relationships, *"Guess Who's Coming to Dinner"*, starring Sydney Poitier, Katherine Hepburn and Spencer Tracy, in which a daughter brings home her black, physician fiancé to meet her white, liberal parents, with surprising results. Furthermore, he uses words and ideas from the poem inscribed on the Statue of Liberty in New York Harbour, the iconic beacon of hope seen by immigrants arriving in the New World. These allusions add a layer of irony to the poem, as well as adding layers of meaning, similar to the poems of Duffy, Turnbull and Heaney.

In exploring **Identity** the poem has similarities with *"Genetics"*, and *"Material"*. It also considers the life of people considered **"Other"** from the point of view of the "Othered", and can be contrasted with *"The Lammas Hireling* and *"Giuseppe"*.

Some commentaries on this poem suggest that the language in which it is written is the *Punglish* of the Immigrants whose arrival in England is the subject of the poem. However, it is far too artful and literary for this to be the case and nothing like the language of the title, nor of Nagra's other poems which use *Punglish* for comic effect, such as *"Singh Song"*, which is included in his eponymous collection. Although, in the last stanza, the narrator ironically identifies himself with the Immigrants whose arrival is described, the poem is written in standard English, although with considerable inventiveness and exuberance. Nagra piles up his description of the immigrant experience of coming to Britain in imaginative and extravagant wordplay, in a *"stream-of-consciousness"* that makes startling associations between ideas and images with a rich use of *neologisms, alliteration, internal rhyme* and *half-rhyme*. This is impressionistic writing, apart from the last stanza, which is relatively plain. It is written in a variety of rhythms, but the pattern in each stanza is similar – a short, opening line, followed by successively lengthening lines which develop the initial premise of each stanza and add a wealth of detail.

Dover has been a gateway to England since the Roman invasion, as it is the closest point to the continent of Europe. Prior to the opening of the Channel Tunnel in 1994, access to the UK from the continent was limited to air and sea travel. Immigrants attempting to enter the UK illegally had to stowaway on cross-channel ferries, often hidden inside coaches, lorries or cars, or risk crossing the English Channel (the world's busiest seaway) in small boats. This last seems the most likely circumstance described in this poem. Attempts to enter the UK via the Tunnel have become a feature of the last 10 years, but a clue to the time-scale of this poem lies in the reference to Tony Blair, Prime Minister from 1997 – 2007, during whose Premiership the final stanza of the poem is set. By this time, the immigrants described in the poem have established themselves as prosperous citizens.

Matthew Arnold's Poem *"Dover Beach"* (1851) is a deeply pessimistic view of England that bewails the loss of Faith. The line quoted by Nagra in context is:

Ah, love, let us be true
to one another! For the world, which seems
To lie before us like a land of dreams,
So various, so beautiful, so new,
Hath really neither joy, nor love, nor light,

Nagra's selective quotation portrays England as the "promised land" and a *"a land of dreams"* – referring to the aspirations of the illegal immigrants who risk their lives to reach it, but also, ironically, to the actuality of what they experience when they arrive. Nagra's poem also refers to *"my love"*, in the last stanza, as he shares his vision of the future with her.

"Stowed" and *"invade"* give a clue as to the circumstance to be described in succeeding stanzas, which is the journey of illegal immigrants to the UK. *"Stowed"* means both *"stored safely"* and a *"Stowaway"* is a person hiding in a vehicle to get free travel. The word *"invade"* also suggests illegality or criminal intent, as seen from the perspective of the inhabitants of the UK. *"Alfresco lash of a diesel-breeze"* refers to the biting fresh air, which smells of the diesel oil powering their little boat. Nagra then seems to amalgamate two images - the foam created by a rough sea, and the spit of passengers on the deck of passing ferries, which seems to be directed towards them. This image of being spat on recurs in the final stanza. *"Gobfuls"* and *"phlegmed""* are both invented words. These passengers are tourists, that can *"come-and-go"* freely, unlike the immigrants. Nagra puns on *"prow'd"*, meaning standing at the front of the boat, and *"proud"*, emphasising their easy (*"cushy"*) entitlement, as does *"lording"* and *"ministered"*, which suggests that they have the authority of the UK Government.

The second stanza recalls the Auden poem, which urges the *"Stranger"* of the title to look at the chalk cliffs of Dover and

79

admire the landscape, imprinting it on his memory. Nagra calls up the sounds of the sea, as does Auden with *"the swaying sound of the sea"* and *"the shingle scrambles after the sucking surf"*. Nagra, more humorously, describes the cries of gulls as *"blarnies"*, an Irish expression from Blarney Castle, near Cork, where there is a stone said to give the power of persuasive speech to those who kiss it. *"Huddled"* is an ironic reference to the words inscribed on the Statue of Liberty, written by Emma Lazarus:

"Give me your tired, your poor,
Your huddled masses yearning to breathe free,
The wretched refuse of your teeming shore."

"Camouflage" suggests that they are still staying hidden as they reach the shore, the crumbling cliffs *"scummed"*, like a dirty white froth, rather than the iconic "White Cliffs". *"Scramming"* is an invented word meaning to *"move quickly"*, as they scramble up the beach. They arrive in pouring rain, as if the sky is pissing on them (*"unbladders"*), the enjambment with *"yobbish"* suggesting that this is what the youths of England do, or would like to do, to these unwanted *"invaders"*. They make their *"escape"* from the beach in a waiting Bedford Van – *"hutched"* suggests being confined like animals.

The new arrivals spend years working illegally, unseen (*"unclocked"* means they are not on any payroll). *"Teemed"* (*swarming with*) again refers to Lazarus's poem, identifying these people with the *"wretched refuse"* and linking to the next stanza: *"swarms of us"*. They live in difficult circumstances, their access to fresh air, in the cities, seems limited – hence the restricted breathing of the *"asthma in parks"*. But the final line of this stanza suggests a shift – that over time their burden ennobles them – they become something else. *"poling sparks"* suggests that they communicate, that they create some kind of kinship with one another and possibly, the native inhabitants of their adopted country.

The *"Swarms"* of immigrants metaphorically work blindly, under-cover of darkness, in the black economy, always at risk of being picked out by the *"moon's spotlight"* of authority. However, they are hopeful (*"banking on"* – a pun) that they will be able to emerge into the *"sun"* of the legitimate economy and find the pot of gold at the end of the *"rainbow"* – a way-out into legitimate employment and acceptance in society. Then they will be able to lift themselves up and out of the darkness, reclaiming their humanity.

The final stanza paints a vision of this wished-for future, where he and his *"love"*, and their fellow immigrants (*"sundry others"* as opposed to *"significant other"*) enjoy all the benefits of Blair's New Labour Britain, owning their own new car, dressed in fashionable clothes, eating at smart restaurants as they see the British do. They will raise their glasses full of champagne (*"charged"* – a pun on using a credit card) and toast their former homelands in the East, all the time speaking their own language which is mixed in with the English of their adopted country (*"chalk"* is a reference to the White Cliffs of Dover). However, this vision is over-laid with another image – just as the passengers on the boats seemed to spit on their boats, so the idea of spitting recurs in the *"flecked"* with white. There is an alternative version of this wished-for life, which is far less accepting of their difference.

Please Hold – Ciaran O'Driscoll

Ciaran O'Driscoll has written that he wrote *"Please Hold"* in anger. *"I found it difficult and a challenge to write [Modernist] poems that made political or social statements, and the obliqueness that ensued often resulted in readers failing to see anything political or social in a poem that I thought had serious, though undercurrent, designs on the world and its wrongs. The only release from this dilemma was anger: when it reached a certain pitch, rage broke through the constraints and actually found imagination in another form – the satirical ...*"[23] The poem is a diatribe against the increasingly impersonal relationship between consumers and providers, and then expands this initial premise into a wider consideration of how we are becoming increasingly dehumanised, ruled by faceless corporations, and losing our sense of **Identity.** This leads to a feeling of helplessness, which may result in violent protest. It is a poem that makes a strong *"political or social"* statement about **the effects of Capitalism** in the early 21st century. The poem also plays with concepts of **Time** and the relationship between the future, present and past, as in *"To My Nine-Year-Old Self"* and *"Material"*.

The poem is written in free verse in a long stanza, which reflects the narrator's circumstance – waiting on the end of a phone line for a response from a bank that he has contacted. He is answered by an automated system. His wife is listening to his mounting frustration, and making (not very helpful) comments to the effect that this is what we have to expect from now on. A number of voices are heard – the poet/narrator's, the wife's, the robot's and the poet's internal commentary on how he feels. Driscoll notably uses *anaphora* (repetition) to convey the mechanistic responses

---

23

http://www.poetryinternationalweb.net/pi/site/poet/item/13165/30/Ciaran-ODriscoll

of the robot, his wife's placid acceptance of the *status quo,* and his own sense of being caught in a system over which he has no control – one with which he is increasingly dissatisfied and becomes increasingly angry. The *mantra*[24] of the wife – *"This is the future"* – interjected at various points in the monologue provide a "tragic chorus" to the action, the meaning subtly changing depending on its context. The effectiveness of this poem arises from our rueful recognition that we have all been there, done that, at some time in our lives, and that we can empathise with the poet – even if the *"robot"* cannot.

The first lines of the poem contain a *paradox*. The first line, spoken by the wife, suggests that the situation in which the poet finds himself is *"the future"* – a future in which machines take over from people, as in countless sci-fi predictions about man's relationship to robots – and that this is what he has to expect. However, the future is already the present, as the poet affirms, suggesting that it is impossible to change what is to come, as it will be already here. He is trapped in a feedback loop.

This idea of a "feedback loop" is developed as he tries to communicate with the "robot". He is given apparently endless choices as to what he might do next – but these do not meet his needs, as he is not being listened to. The disconnect between the *"robot"* and the caller is evident from the inappropriate responses that it makes to his answers to its questions. These have been designed to make the caller feel valued, but do the exact opposite by revealing its lack of comprehension and its absence of empathy. Ironically, it enthuses over the mechanistic (the numbers) not the person. The poet juxtaposes the answers and responses for satirical effect: *"wonderful telephone number/great account number"*. In contrast, the poet has quickly gone from referring to it as *"a robot"* to *"him"*.

---

[24] A *mantra* is a chant with repeated phrases

The italicisation of *"my"* shows the poet trying to hang on to his sense of self – the robot/bank is appropriating his account, taking his money to pay for a robot which fails to deliver what he needs – *"doing nothing"*. This causes him to shout out loud at the phone – as if it could a) hear him or b) will respond. This is a very human reaction to an intractable problem. The repeated response – *"Wonderful"* – shows the gulf between them. The wife's repeated *"This is the future"* begins to sound, in itself, robotic; it is the voice of someone who appears to have given up the struggle a long time ago.

The robot offers further Options, all of which are equally unhelpful. The poet's screamed attempt to get through to a *"real"* person, an Agent, (even though he suspects that this will be equally useless) is thwarted by being *"cut off"*, as if the robot has taken offence at being rejected – an irony in itself. The word *"Agent"* is also dehumanising – it suggests that the person lacks autonomy, acting merely on instructions from an unseen "boss". The interjection by the wife this time seems a comment on the poet's helplessness. He is given options, the appearance of freedom, but is actually trapped.

The poet appears to redial and this time is put on hold, listening to the looped recorded music. The music is by Mozart, and is usually translated *"A Little Night-music"* (as in the title of Sondheim's musical). However, its more literal translation is *"A Little Serenade"*, meaning a composition written in honour of someone – which adds a layer of irony to the choice, as the poet is feeling far from special. In fact, his growing frustration at the continuous looping of the recording and repeated injunction to *"Please hold"*, results in a violent expletive, which is comic for its contrast with the classical restraint of this very famous, and beloved, piece of music: *"Eine fucking Kleine Nachtmusik"*.

The next line is *bathos* – an understatement for comic effect. The poet's anger is deflated by the robot's *tour de force* of transferring the caller from one part of the "system" to another part of the same system – effectively, *"to himself"*. The use of the standard phrase *"your call is important to us"* further points up the absurdity of what is happening. The robot/system is now effectively talking to itself about itself, and lying about itself in the process. Everything that has happened up to this point has demonstrated to the caller that he is anything but *"important"*. *"My translator"* is his inner self, that bit of him that is, as yet, not caught up in the conspiracy of the machines. Now, the wife's words sound like a note of doom.

However, his internal monologue suggests a more radical solution to his conundrum, taking the theme of the poem beyond the immediate circumstance of a phone call to a bank, to a comment on the value put on people by society as a whole – or rather, those parts of it which control a Capitalist economic system. He suggests that the *"only way you can now meet your needs/is by looting"* – smashing the existing system and taking what you need by force. This makes the poem prescient. It was written in 2008, as the height of the financial crisis; in 2011, following the shooting of an (arguably) unarmed black man in North London, localised civil unrest quickly escalated, leading to widespread rioting and looting across the Capital, and other major cities. It was the worst riot in London for decades and has been attributed to many factors, including a feeling of disenfranchisement caused by the economic downturn, as well as racial tensions. The robot's comment *"Wonderful"* is seen as doubly chilling in this context. Not only does it not understand the forces operating on the caller, but it does not, and cannot, care about the possible outcomes.

The final *tercet* acts as a commentary or refrain. The poet plays with the robot's repeated message, using rhyme to create an increasing feeling of helplessness. *"Please hold/grow old/grow cold"* suggests that, given long enough, the caller (we) will get used to this new order and lose our anger, accepting what we have been given. The "robot" system is still holding to the pretence of working for us with the *"Please"*. However, it then becomes an injunction: *"Please do what you're told"*, denying us the right to challenge. *"Grow old. Grow cold"* have now lost the placatory *"Please"* and become a command. It is the robot which now tells us *"This is the future"* and instructs us to *"hang on"* – indefinitely.

This is another poem, like *"From the Journal..."* and *"Please Hold"*, in which questions remain unanswered about a future that is uncertain. This is perhaps in contrast to those written by the women in this selection who see continuity and surety in the love between parents and children, or in loving relationships.

On Her Blindness – Adam Thorpe

The poem's title is a reference to the *sonnet* by John Milton (1608-1674) *"On His Blindness"*. Milton, the writer of the great Epic poem *"Paradise Lost"* (1667), which describes the Fall of Man and the expulsion from the garden of Eden, went blind in 1654 and from then on relied on an *amanuensis* (scribe) to whom he dictated his works, including the twelve book *"Paradise Lost"* and the subsequent four book *"Paradise Regained"*, as well as countless prose tracts. The message of his *sonnet* is to accept blindness with stoicism and contains the famous last line: *"They also serve who only stand and wait."*

Thorpe's is another poem that could be considered an *elegy*, written on the occasion of his mother's death, but focusing on her late-life blindness. Other *elegies* in the selection include *"Material"*, and *"Effects"*. Like these, the poem is about **the relationship between children and parents** but also about **Identity** and the loss of it in old age, as disability and death encroach on the sense of self.

The poem is written predominantly in *"blank verse"* – un-rhyming couplets of *iambic pentametre*. This may well be a homage to Milton. "Blank verse", until Milton, was associated solely with drama (as in Shakespeare). Unrhymed verse in poetry was unusual, as was playing around with the positioning of the *caesura* (the break or stop in a line) and the use of *enjambment* to link ideas across successive lines, varying the stress. Thorpe's poem is notable for the use of all these techniques, creating a confiding, conversational tone, juxtaposing ideas in surprising ways as he reflects on his mother's affliction, her reaction to it and his own, painful, response to her incapacity and eventual death. The tone shifts between pragmatism, tenderness, pain, grief and acceptance.

The opening three couplets throw down a challenge, as it were, to both the stoicism of Milton, and the "politically correct". His mother *"can't bear being blind"*. This is not something that those, like Milton, who advocate "grin and bear it" (the stoic response *"bear it/like a Roman"*), nor those who celebrate disability (*"find joy"*) want to hear. He is uncompromising, as she is, and tells it for what it is to her: a *"catastrophic/ handicap"*.

He recounts a painful episode in a Paris restaurant, where they went when blindness was new to her (*"still not finding/the food on her plate"*), where she admits to contemplating suicide. The uncompromising retelling of this incident is heightened by the use of the *enjambment* across the stanzas and couplets: *"finding/the food"*, *"try it/in a pitch-black room"*, *"I'd bump/myself off"*. These unexpected juxtapositions leave the reader constantly wrong-footed, off-balance, like a blind person feeling their way in an unfamiliar room. There is also something very poignant in the use of her son's name, *"Adam"*, as she confides her darkest thoughts to him and in his shame-faced admittance that he has no adequate response to her expression of her pain: *"inadequate; the locked in son"*, as unable to express his emotions as much as she is *"locked-in"* to her blindness.

Both his father and he respond to the wife and mother's new circumstance with a lack of sentimentality, and even humour, as a ward against despair. Her determination to *"keep her dignity"* is respected, even when he describes her, with intended *bathos*[25], as *"bumping...like a dodgem"*. Contrary to popular myth, her blindness does not result in improvement in her other senses, nor the development of a "sixth sense" (*"built-in compass"*) that enables her to find her way around safely.

---

[25] *Bathos* is a comic effect created by an anti-climax; here, contrasting serious subject matter with an amusing image.

Her coping strategy emerges in the next stanzas. She pretends to see when she cannot, not wishing to disappoint the grandchildren and smiling when they show her their "*latest drawing*" or "*new toy*". There are times when he and his father could forget that her gradually deteriorating sight has ended in total blindness, in the uncompromising *simile* "*blank as stone*".

Her son recalls her "*long, /slow slide*" into blindness, his mother denying the reality – continuing to drive, looking at art and films, and finally pretending to watch "*television/while looking the wrong way.*" Again, the apparent positivity of the drive and continuing pleasurable visits is brutally undercut by the *enjambment* across the stanza which reveals the awful reality and sadness of her conditions and the extent of her denial.

The poet recalls her last weeks alive in hospital, the autumn weather glorious, the leaves golden on the trees and the ground. "*royal*" is a *metaphor* for these golden leaves. The "*of course*" is ironic – *pathetic fallacy*[26] does not work in real life. He starts to describe the colours to his mother, but she remains in denial to the last: "*staring at nothing*" she pretends she can see the autumn colours for herself. Or can she in her memory? Is there some ambiguity here suggesting that the son knows less about her thoughts than he thinks?

Now that she is dead, she is truly sightless and all pretence is over. All the father and son can do, if they choose, is to believe in an after-life where she is restored as she was in life, before her blindness, and is watching over them.

---

[26] *Pathetic fallacy* (literally "*false feeling*") is a device which mirrors human emotions in the natural world, as if it is in sympathy.

On a Grayson Perry Urn – Tim Turnbull

Grayson Perry is a 21st century artist, who might have been described as *"avant garde"* in his early career but now is very much part of the art establishment, having won the Turner Prize in 2003 and the CBE in 2013. He had a difficult and fractured childhood, becoming estranged from most of his family by his late teens through family break-down, and because he is a transvestite, his alter ego being a woman called Claire. Perry produces pots which depict scenes from modern life, just as the Greeks produced vases and urns for carrying liquids showing everyday scenes and stories from mythology. In this poem, Ted Turnbull has produced a *pastiche* - a version with an amusing intent - of John Keats' (1795 – 1821) poem "*Ode to a Grecian Urn*", updating it for a modern reader. Whilst it is possible to enjoy this poem without knowing the Keats original, there seems little doubt that Turnbull expects his readers to have at least some familiarity with it. Much of the point of *pastiche* is lost without the comparison, as the humour and cleverness lies in the moments of recognition of how the original has been subverted. Keats' *"Ode"*, with a commentary, has been added at the end and, ideally, should be read before the Turnbull to appreciate how he has used his model.

Turnbull's poem, like Keats', considers *aesthetics*, the perception of **Truth** and **Beauty** – are they absolutes, or do they lie in *"the eye of the beholder"*? This provides an interesting links to *"Eat Me"*. Like Keats' poem, it dwells on concepts of **Time** and **History** and our perceptions of them. In the effects of **Time** it links with *"To My Nine-Year-Old Self"* and **History** links to *"History"*. The subject matter of the Urn provides a **social commentary** on the lives of people in the early 21st century, as in *"Please Hold..."*.

An *ode* is a lyric poem with its origins in Ancient Greece, where it was set to music. It is addressed in praise of an object, or person, which is then expanded to reflect on an abstract concept – here, the nature of truth and beauty. Keats famously wrote Odes "*To Autumn*", "*To Melancholy*", and "*To a Nightingale*." Like Keats' "*Ode*", it is written in *iambic pentametre* and Turnbull keeps to the same structure as Keats - five stanzas of ten lines with a rhyming scheme *ababcde(dce)*. The *triplet* may vary between *dce/ced*. Turnbull also keeps to the same ordering of his argument as Keats over the five stanzas. For a modern poem, not only is the form deliberately "traditional," but the use of poetic techniques - *alliteration, assonance, enjambment, caesura* - are as much features of Turnbull's poem as of Keats'.

Turnbull opens his poem, like Keats, with a direct address to the subject of the ode, the Urn, but whereas Keats' tone is reverent, ("*Thou still, unravis'd bride*"), Turnbull uses the vernacular ("*Hello! What's all this here?*"). At first, the tone and attitude with which Turnbull approaches his subject seems sarcastic, even rude, about the pot, the artist and the subject matter of the decoration. The pot is a "*kitschy*" vase - a derogatory term for something clever and popular but lacking artistic merit - and Perry himself, with a reference to his cross-dressing, is sneeringly described as a "*Shirley Temple manqué*" or wannabe. Shirley Temple was a child-star of the 1930s who wore her hair in ringlets, as does Perry when Claire. The term "*knocked out*" suggests that these pots are made quickly and carelessly, unlike the artistry that is associated with a Greek antique pottery. This is clearly tongue-in-cheek, as a Grayson Perry vase is made using exceptionally difficult and elaborate techniques to decorate and glaze, and can sell for more than £100,000. However, Turnbull's irreverent tone is part of his message – the Greek vases that we see now as objects of artistic beauty were, in fact, every-day, utilitarian objects used in the kitchen to carry liquids. They were not intended to be seen primarily as works of art, although great care was taken to decorate them. Turnbull is commenting on how our perceptions of what is beautiful, and valuable, changes with time. He is being ironic in referring to Grayson Perry's pots as similarly ordinary pieces, because they are created as original works of art. Art is imitating Life.

The Perry vase, like Keats', tells stories of its time. On Perry's Urn, the subjects of the decoration are modern, urban,"*youf*", an updated version of Keats' pastoral *"men... and maidens"*. Note the words *"delineated"* and later, *"evocation"*. This is not vernacular, but Latinate, meaning literally *"drawn with lines"*, which is how the case is decorated, and to *"call out"*. Turnbull frequently switches between the two modes of language, and by doing so draws both parallels and distinctions between his and Keats' poetic style and his approach to his subject matter. Notice also the alliteration of *"kids, cars, crap"*. This poem is deceptively written. Although Turnbull uses a modern vernacular, at times, the poem is actually highly crafted in its use of poetic techniques. Turnbull appears to undercut the "classicism" of poetry like Keats', but shows that he is writing in the same tradition, just as Perry's vase follows that of the Greeks.

The "youf" are negatively described as "*louts*" and firmly placed as urbanites (as opposed to the pastoral setting of Keats) of a particular social class. Burberry is a very expensive, high-end brand, which is frequently ripped off and sold in markets as the real thing and hence affordable by these young men who have nothing better to do than drive around in their *"motors"* – a word for "cars" which is usually used by working class men. *"Flail"* literally means *"beat with a flail"*, a tool for threshing corn. It is synonymous with hard work – something which, Turnbull ironically implies, these young men do not do. Each of their hometowns (*"Manchester/Motherwell/Slough"*) is, or has been, a by-word for urban blight, social deprivation and youth disaffection. "*Queen's Highway*" is a colloquial expression for "road". Turnbull suggests that these lives, stylised on the vase, can be "*conjured*" (brought to life) without prompting a back-lash in the *Daily Express*, a right-wing tabloid which is usually quick to jump at the chance of demonising "idle layabouts". Like the decoration on Keats' vase, these are pictures, not real and therefore silent and harmless.

In stanza two, there is an increasingly lyrical tone to the writing, as the poet acknowledges the power of the "pot" to evoke a particular moment in place and time and to impart beauty to even the most mundane of subjects. This stanza focuses on the sounds of cars and music on the radio, (*Garage* and *house*) whereas Keats focuses on "*pipes and timbrels*". Turnbull conjures up the sound of the "*motors*", ("*throaty roar*", "*joyful throb*") and the cries of their girl passengers. Note the *eye-rhyme* in *throaty, roar*, and the *assonance* on "*screech/squeals*", as well as the Latinate "*educe*" (meaning "to draw out").

Although the Urn can help us imagine the noise of the cars and music, of the engines at full throttle, the girls screaming excitedly, yet we can feel "*calm*" as these are merely painted pictures, frozen in time. "*no harm*" can come to them. Turnbull uses *enjambment* and *caesura*, placing the emphasis on the "peril" they are in and then balancing with the "safety" ("*appreciate/the peril, wheels/will not lose traction, no harm/befall*. This is Keats' moment when he declares "*She cannot fade*".

The link to the third stanza is made with the *enjambment* "*stay out late/forever*", echoing Keats' description of the lovers "*for ever panting...*" This stanza focuses on sex and drugs. The frequent *enjambment* and short phrases propels the verse forward with increasing urgency. Turnbull is mirroring Keats' description of the young men chasing the maidens around the vase – girls that they will never catch, the prelude to sex that will never happen, just as Turnbull's youth will never have to go home to bed and worry about getting up for work next day. The description of their sexual exploits is graphic and uncompromising, using the language of his subjects: "*buff/geezer/given head*". Their sexual potency is conveyed in "*charged with pulsing juice/ fills every pair/never… deflated*". There is a directness in his foretelling of the possible outcome of the behaviour of the real subjects of Perry's vase - contracting an STI - as Turnbull, of course, can see into the future of these real young men and women. This mirrors, but also, in its modern realism, contrasts with Keats' Romantic interpretation, that the men and women on his urn, "*forever panting and forever young*", will never know the pains of love as he has known, the "*Burning forehead and a parching tongue*".

The fourth stanza is a variation of the scene of sacrifice on Keats' urn. It opens with an injunction to "*Now see*" as a procession of young men, drinking beer, line the streets to watch the boys in their cars perform tricks ("*burn-outs and donut Os*"), watched by the neighbours hidden behind their lace curtains. Although this stanza appears to return to a harsher tone, there is a suggestion that at least the activities of these boys are life-affirming, in contrast to the "*bleached tarmac of dead suburban streets*" and the onlookers behind the curtains, too old or too cynical to take part themselves, or appreciate the thrill. There is also sympathy in the acknowledgement that quiet streets are for those that can afford them, making further social comment. These "*dead streets*" are a mirror of Keats' deserted town.

In the last stanza, Turnbull, like Keats, addresses the Urn with an apparent return to the sarcasm of the first stanza. Whereas Keats addresses the Urn as "*Fair attitude!*", Turnbull calls it a "*garish crock*", an over-decorated, vulgar, worthless pot. But like Keats, Turnbull is reflecting how our perception of an object's beauty is affected by the passage of time - the mundane becomes the extraordinary with time and distance. There is humour in the euphemism of *"we're long in the box"* as he acknowledges that whereas these images are fixed for all time, we are doomed to mortality.

Unlike Keats' *Ode*, however, Turnbull's *"Ode…"* ends on a question - although the question mark is missing. He wonders whether, in the distant future (*"sun a little colder"*) a poet will look back on these images immortalised on the pot and ask the same question that Keats, and now he, has asked. Will they see this time as one of freedom and joy, where things were not simply black and white; when there is no such thing as absolute truth? Will they think it a happier time, when truth was not so easy to define and beauty was in the eye of the beholder? This is a modern take on Keats' *"Beauty is Truth"*. For Keats, beauty is an absolute – just as the Grecian Urn is an absolute – but for the modern world, perhaps, definitions are less fixed.

The poet seems to end ambiguously, whereas Keats' makes a clear statement (if you accept the usual interpretation and do not dismiss it as meaningless). The apparently judgemental attitude of Turnbull towards the young people depicted on the one hand suggests that their lifestyle lacks meaning, and hence worth and that a return to absolutes is preferable. On the other, there are moments of sympathy and even tenderness, which suggests that all lives are to be celebrated and that everything is relative. Similarly, the terms with which the pot is addressed (*"kitsch"*, *"crock"*) suggests that it has no intrinsic value – indeed, that it has less than Keats' urn as it was not made for a purpose – and yet the poet knows how "valuable" the "crock" is in this modern world – again, suggesting relativity and that "worth", not just beauty, lies in the eye of the beholder. The poet may also be commenting on the media's attitude to the depiction of men and women today.

It is also a comment, of course, on his own poem, as Turnbull has taken an iconic poem and made a *pastiche*, a humorous adaptation, rather like Grayson Perry has hijacked the Greek vase for his own subversive purposes, reinterpreting it for a modern audience.

Ode to a Grecian Urn – John Keats

Thou still unravish'd bride of quietness,
Thou foster-child of silence and slow time,
Sylvan historian, who canst thus express
A flowery tale more sweetly than our rhyme:
What leaf-fring'd legend haunts about thy shape
Of deities or mortals, or of both,
In Tempe or the dales of Arcady?
What men or gods are these? What maidens loth?
What mad pursuit? What struggle to escape?
What pipes and timbrels? What wild ecstasy?

The whole poem is addressed to the Urn. It is best to imagine you, the reader, watching and listening to Keats as he walks around examining the urn, and muses on what meaning it holds for us. He is contemplating how it has survived, unbroken, (*"unravish'd"*) for thousands of years, quietly revealing the lives of Greek Gods and mortals. The scene on the urn is possibly one of a Dionysian orgy, a celebration to the God of Music and Wine, showing *"men or gods"* chasing young women to the sounds of music and the sacrifice of a bull to the God.

Heard melodies are sweet, but those unheard
Are sweeter; therefore, ye soft pipes, play on;
Not to the sensual ear, but, more endear'd,
Pipe to the spirit ditties of no tone:
Fair youth, beneath the trees, thou canst not leave
Thy song, nor ever can those trees be bare;
Bold Lover, never, never canst thou kiss,
Though winning near the goal yet, do not grieve;
She cannot fade, though thou hast not thy bliss,
For ever wilt thou love, and she be fair!

The second stanza addresses the scenes of music-making and the "lovers". Keats' is reconciled to being unable to hear the music being played by claiming that the music of the *"spirit"*, unheard, is sweeter. By this, he could be referring to the creative process, or to the *"music of the spheres"*, the harmony that was believed in pre-scientific times to exist between cosmic bodies – a relationship that was likened to music, although unheard. He continues with images of everlasting youth – the "youth" piping beneath the trees which are forever in green leaf, the young man chasing the girl he will never catch. The consolation for never realising their goal is that he will be in love forever and she will always *"be fair!"* and never age.

Ah, happy, happy boughs! that cannot shed
    Your leaves, nor ever bid the Spring adieu;
And, happy melodist, unwearied,
    For ever piping songs for ever new;
More happy love! more happy, happy love!
    For ever warm and still to be enjoy'd,
        For ever panting, and for ever young;
All breathing human passion far above,
    That leaves a heart high-sorrowful and cloy'd,
        A burning forehead, and a parching tongue.

Stanza three continues on the theme of time being frozen and declares that this is a *"happy"* circumstance. This timeless and enduring love is better than the mortal experience of love which ends in sadness, is spoiled and gives the lover symptoms as if of an illness.

Who are these coming to the sacrifice?
    To what green altar, O mysterious priest,
Lead'st thou that heifer lowing at the skies,
    And all her silken flanks with garlands drest?
What little town by river or sea shore,

Or mountain-built with peaceful citadel,
    Is emptied of this folk, this pious morn?
And, little town, thy streets for evermore
    Will silent be; and not a soul to tell
        Why thou art desolate, can e'er return.

The fourth stanza looks at the scenes of a sacrifice on the vase. *"Drest"* is an archaic spelling of *"dressed"* – the cow being led to the sacrifice is decorated with flowers. Keats imagines the towns being emptied as the people come and follow the procession to the God's shrine. He reflects that they will never return to the now empty town, and that no-one will be able to explain what happened to make it deserted.

O Attic shape! Fair attitude! with brede
    Of marble men and maidens overwrought,
With forest branches and the trodden weed;
    Thou, silent form, dost tease us out of thought
As doth eternity: Cold Pastoral!
    When old age shall this generation waste,
        Thou shalt remain, in midst of other woe
Than ours, a friend to man, to whom thou say'st,
    "Beauty is truth, truth beauty, — that is all
        Ye know on earth, and all ye need to know."

In the final stanza, he is addressing the urn directly once again. *"Attic"* means "Ancient Greek" and *"brede"* means "embroidered" or "decorated". He is telling the urn that by looking at it and the stories it tells, he is being led to reflect, in this poem, on the nature of our life (*"tease us out of thought"*) as do thoughts of the meaning of *"eternity"*. The scene before him is *"cold"* because it is unchanging and lifeless, but it has a message for we mortals who will die, while it remains. Keats ends with the vase giving its message to us directly. The urn is *"replying"* to Keats' musings on mortality. It is a quote within a quote – the *"Beauty is truth, truth beauty"* was written by a famous artist, Sir Joshua Reynolds, affirming that the meaning of our lives can be seen in beautiful things – art, poetry, music. So, the urn is repeating this (speaking of itself, as it were, as a beautiful object) and then saying that beauty and truth are all we have and all we need to understand our lives.

There is considerable amount of debate about what these lines actually mean – from that given above to being absolutely meaningless.

Links, Connections and Tackling the Unseen Poem

Making "links and connections" and tackling the Unseen Poem

The exam question

The exam question will give you a *"theme"* to discuss as a guide to which aspects of the poem(s) they want you to focus on. They may use the word *"Compare"*; the mark scheme refers only to making *"effective connections"* with *"a discriminating use of examples"* at the highest band.

Where possible, these links and connections should be made to each poem throughout the essay, alternating between the two, for the highest marks. The examiners are less keen on one analysis followed by another, unless there is clear cross-referencing and/or there is a clearly comparative paragraph at the beginning and at the end.

What is happening in the poem?

The first task is to understand *"What is happening in the poem?"* Unless you understand this, your analysis will be meaningless. Make sure you understand what the story, incident, event or imaginative idea is that has prompted the poet to write the poem. No poem exists in a vacuum – there is always a reason for writing it. Find that reason – the inspiration which leads to the poem.

The first "link or connection" to be made is to summarise, briefly, the "story" of each poem *and how this relates to the theme of the question*. This is the first response to *"How"* the poet has approached his subject matter. It is the framework around which he hangs his ideas. It is suggested that you do this in your first paragraph. It also reassures the Examiner that your analysis is not starting from an erroneous base.

Form, structure and language

A poem may have many ideas in it. Your task is to explain **how the poet has used form, structure and language to explore the theme which is the focus of the question**. Below are some of the features of the poems that you can choose to explore, both when making links and connections between the prescribed poem and one other from the *Poems of the Decade* at AS Level, AND when linking the Unseen poem with one of the prescribed poems at A Level.

Remember that the highest marks are given when the analysis of form, structure and language is related to meaning and to the theme under discussion. Fewer marks are given for merely identifying techniques in isolation from meaning. The commentaries on the poems show you how to do this.

It is important that you use *"examples"* (quotes) to illustrate your argument. Never make a comment about how the poet has approached his subject without an example to illustrate. You should also ***never use a quote without then going on to talk about the quote*** itself, analysing any structural or language features in depth and ***relating this to the effect on the reader***. This ensures that you are covering the assessment objective AO2 – *"showing a critical understanding of the writer's craft."*

Theme	The question will focus on a theme. Some key themes have been identified in the commentary on the texts. Choose poems which can be linked thematically as a first choice for linking and connecting. Trying to link poems "because you know them" is not a good plan.
Narrative Voice	Who is speaking in the poem? Is it the poet, or is he speaking through someone else? Is there more than one *voice*? The narrative voice is the person who is speaking in the poem. It may be the poet (many of the poems are autobiographical) or a *persona* – an imagined speaker, as in a *dramatic monologue*. Or it may be the poet simply talking to us about an idea that he/she wishes to explore. **What does the choice of narrative voice tell us about the poet's approach to his theme or about the theme itself?**
Form	Is the poem written in a named poetic form, such as *sonnet, ode, elegy, ballad*? Does the poem reference an existing work? Is it a *pastiche* or in a particular poetic tradition? **What does the choice of form tell you about the subject matter or the attitude of the poet?**
Structure	How is the poem arranged on the page? How many lines are there in a stanza? How is the story arranged around these lines? What is the subject matter of each stanza? In what order has the story or happening been told to us? Are there shifts in time or place? Is there a regular rhythm? If so, what is this rhythm? Is there a regular rhyme scheme? Are *full rhymes, half-rhymes* and *eye-rhymes* used? Are the lines *end-stopped* – does the meaning

	follow the rhyme and complete at the end of each rhymed line?
	Does the poet use *enjambment* and *caesura* to vary the pace of the line and create a looser structure within a rigid one? What does this say about the subject matter or the poet's attitude to his subject?
	Is it in free verse, with no discernible regular rhyme or rhythm?
	How has the poet chosen where to end the lines?
	How does the choice and use of structure relate to meaning and what is the effect on the reader?
Language	Is the language formal or informal?
	Does it sound conversational, confiding, reminiscent, musing, purposeful...?
	What is the tone – sorrowful, regretful, angry, puzzled, triumphant...?
	What is the proportion of vernacular (words of common speech) to Latinate (polysyllabic, Latin derivations, "difficult")?
	Is the language descriptive, factual, plain, colloquial ...?
	Is the language literal, or does it have many *similes* and *metaphors*, or *personification*?
	What kinds of *imagery* are used? Religious, naturalistic, mechanistic...?
	Are there particular words used which are unusual? Archaic, dialect, slang ...?
	Are there any unusual words in the context of the whole?
	How does the choice and use of language relate to meaning and what is the effect on the reader?

.

Printed in Great Britain
by Amazon